Praise for Burning the Ships

"When Marshall Phelps took the job at Microsoft in 2003, many in the industry believed he was on a fool's errand. The task of helping to transform the culture and business practices of Microsoft through the use of its intellectual property seemed impossible. *Burning the Ships* proves that Marshall is the unchallenged master in designing creative uses of intellectual property to enhance business performance. And through his collaboration with David Kline, they've accomplished something equally unique: a thoroughly entertaining and informative 'can't wait to get to the next page' read."

—Daniel McCurdy
Chairman, Patent Freedom

"*Burning the Ships* offers a dramatic insider's account of how Microsoft used intellectual property to remake its business strategy and embrace the open source movement and the new open innovation world—with real-world benefits for large enterprise customers and chief information officers everywhere."

—Jim Noble
Chairman, World BPO Forum
Past President, Society for Information Management

"When Marshall Phelps talks about intellectual property strategy, business leaders would be wise to listen closely. More than anyone else in business today, Marshall understands how open innovation has changed the rules of the IP strategy game. It's time we learned the new rules!"

—Ruud J. Peters
CEO, Philips Intellectual Property
Executive Vice President, Philips International

"It's easy to talk open innovation and collaboration but extremely difficult to actually implement it in any company. Phelps and Kline bring to life the painful realities and unexpected rewards of embracing this change in Microsoft. The important story, though, is not the challenge of changing course, but that other companies can reap similar benefits of accelerated innovation, stronger partnerships, and better corporate image by 'burning the ships.' Read it and 'start a fire.'"

> —Jeffrey D. Weedman
> Vice President, External Business Development
> Procter & Gamble

"Through the power of example and compelling firsthand accounts, the authors have conveyed many practical insights about how intellectual property can be harnessed in new and creative ways to achieve overall business objectives and enable new collaborations once considered unthinkable. This book is extremely readable and refreshingly devoid of the abstract jargon and theoretical frameworks plaguing many works on IP management."

> —Daniel M. McGavock
> Vice President and Intellectual Property Practice Leader
> CRA International, Inc.

"*Burning the Ships* is the dramatic story of how Microsoft learned to collaborate for open innovation by using intellectual property to develop new corporate strategies."

> —Hisamitsu Arai
> Former Commissioner, Japan Patent Office
> Former Cabinet Member, Secretary General,
> Japan's Intellectual Property Secretariat
> CEO of Tokyo Small and Medium Business
> Investment Organization

"*Burning the Ships* gives a rare insider perspective on the thought processes behind the intellectual property strategies of companies like Microsoft and IBM. It offers revealing insights to practitioners in the field."

—Willy Shih
Professor of Management Practice
Harvard Business School

"Marshall Phelps is *the* internationally recognized leader in the use of intellectual property as a strategic corporate asset. He recognizes that long-term survival in the constantly evolving information technology industry requires a flexible and nuanced intellectual property policy. *Burning the Ships* shows business leaders how to develop one for today's open innovation environment."

—Masanobu Katoh
Corporate Vice President
Senior Vice President, Global Business Group
(in charge of North America)
Fujitsu Limited

"Marshall Phelps is the principal architect of two dramatically different but equally compelling examples—one at IBM and one at Microsoft—of how intellectual property can be a transformational business tool when thoughtfully used to drive business strategy. It is a critically important message that he and David Kline make understandable to any company seeking to learn how it is done."

—Don Davis
Managing Director
Commercial Strategy, LLC

"Once again a book involving David Kline—this time in partnership with the formidable Marshall Phelps—has moved the IP revolution forward. The story of Microsoft's open innovation efforts, led by Phelps, is fascinating and informative. But the book also provides a whole new level of understanding of the necessity of managing and fully leveraging intellectual property as a strategic class of business assets. Intelligent companies that follow this example will find that they can grow in ways not previously contemplated."

—Peter Ackerman
CEO, Innovation Asset Group

Burning the Ships

Intellectual Property and the Transformation of Microsoft

Marshall Phelps
David Kline

WILEY

John Wiley & Sons, Inc.

Published by John Wiley & Sons, Inc., Hoboken, New Jersey.
Published simultaneously in Canada.

For general information on our other products and services, or technical support, please contact our Customer Care Department within the United States at 800-762-2974, outside the United States at 317-572-3993 or fax 317-572-4002.

Wiley also publishes its books in a variety of electronic formats. Some content that appears in print may not be available in electronic books.

For more information about Wiley products, visit our Web site at http://www.wiley.com.

Library of Congress Cataloging-in-Publication Data

Phelps, Marshall.
   Burning the ships : intellectual property and the transformation of Microsoft / Marshall Phelps, David Kline.
        p. cm.
   Includes index.
   ISBN 978-0-470-43215-0 (cloth)
    1. Microsoft Corporation.   2. Computer software—United States—Patents.
 I. Kline, David, 1950–   II. Title.
   KF3133.C65P47 2009
   346.7304'86—dc22   2009000832

Printed in the United States of America

10 9 8 7 6 5 4 3 2 1

To Eileen Phelps and Sarah Kline

Contents

"For us, it was the equivalent of Cortez burning his ships at the shores of the New World. There would be no turning back."
—Brad Smith
General Counsel, Microsoft

About the Authors

Marshall Phelps is Microsoft's corporate vice president for intellectual property policy and strategy and is responsible for setting the global intellectual property strategies and policies for the company. He also works with governments, other companies in the technology industry, and outside institutions to broaden awareness of intellectual property issues.

Before transitioning to his current position in 2006, Phelps served as the deputy general counsel for intellectual property in Microsoft's Legal & Corporate Affairs group, where he supervised Microsoft's intellectual property groups, including those responsible for trademarks, trade secrets, patents, licensing, standards, and copyrights. He oversaw the company's management of its intellectual property portfolio, helping to grow the patent portfolio to approximately 55,000 issued and pending patents worldwide today.

Phelps joined Microsoft in June 2003 after a 28-year career at IBM Corp., where he served as vice president for intellectual property and licensing. Phelps was instrumental in IBM's standards, telecommunications policy, industry relations, patent licensing program, and intellectual property portfolio development. Phelps also helped establish IBM's Asia Pacific headquarters in Tokyo and served as the company's director of government relations in Washington, D.C.

Upon retiring from IBM in 2000, he spent two years as chairman and chief executive officer of Spencer Trask Intellectual Capital Company LLC, which specialized in spinoffs from major corporations such as Motorola Inc., Lockheed Martin Corp. and IBM.

Marshall Phelps is also an advisor on intellectual property to the Japanese government, and executive in residence at Duke University's Fuqua School of Business. He holds a bachelor of arts degree from Muskingum College, a master of science degree from Stanford Graduate School of Business, and a doctorate from Cornell Law School.

Phelps was elected to the initial class of the Intellectual Property Hall of Fame in 2006. He may be reached at mphelps@microsoft.com.

David Kline is a journalist, author, and intellectual property consultant who has earned a reputation for his unique ability to demystify complex IP issues and explain them in a clear and relevant manner to a broad business audience. His best-selling 2000 book, *Rembrandts in the Attic* from Harvard Business School Press, is considered a seminal work in the field of intellectual property strategy within corporate America.

As a journalist, Kline has covered some of the world's most dramatic stories for the *New York Times, Christian Science Monitor, NBC* and *CBS News*, the *Atlantic, Rolling Stone, Wired,* and other major media. The first Western reporter to go behind the battle lines in Afghanistan in the 1979 to report on the developing anti-Soviet resistance war, Kline was nominated for a Pulitzer Prize in international reporting by the *Christian Science Monitor* that year and covered the war for a variety of major media over the next eight years. He was also the first reporter to uncover the 1983 famine in Ethiopia, as well as the first to document the failure of the U.S. drug war against the Bolivian "Coca Nostra" in the mid-1980s.

A highly regarded business writer, Kline has also written for the *Harvard Business Review, Sloan Management Review*, and *Strategy + Business*—three of the most prestigious U.S. management journals—as well as for *Chief Executive, Business2.0, Wired*, and other business and technology publications. He served as the "Market Forces" columnist for *Wired's* early online magazine, *HotWired,* and the "NetProfits" columnist for the former *Upside* magazine. Kline has also been a commentator on public radio's "Marketplace" business show as well as a frequent speaker before business audiences.

In addition to *Rembrandts in the Attic,* Kline is also the author of *Road Warriors: Dreams and Nightmares Along the Information Highway* (Dutton, 1995), and *Blog! How the Newest Media Revolution Is Changing Politics, Business, and Culture* (CDS, October, 2005). He may be reached at dkline@well.com.

Acknowledgments

T his book was a bear to write. But thankfully, a great many people helped us to wrestle it into submission by sharing their thoughts and insights, brainstorming about the future, helping to explain what might otherwise have been inscrutable technological issues, digging deep into old files for critical facts or the dates of crucial events, and in general being forthright and often brilliant in their criticisms and suggestions.

Put another way, to even attempt to write a book about a subject as complex and multifaceted as the transformation of Microsoft requires more in the way of advice and counsel, criticism and support, than the casual reader might suppose. We are grateful for everyone's help.

At the same time, we want to make it perfectly clear that any errors, omissions, or stupidities in this book are ours and ours alone.

Among the many people inside and outside Microsoft who gave so generously of their time and wisdom to this project, we wish to thank in particular (but in no particular order) the following:

Brad Smith, Bill Gates, Nathan Myhrvold, Horacio Gutierrez, Lori Harnick, Mike Marinello, Susan Hauser, David Kaefer, Anne Kelley, Tanya Moore, Lisa Tanzi, Bart Eppenauer, John Weresh, Ken Lustig, Marty Shively, Tom Robertson, Tom Rubin, David Harnett, Dan'l Lewin, Jason Matusow, Atsushi "Yoshi" Yoshida, Susan Mann, George Zinn, Mark Murray, Mike Ensing, Tricia Payer, Tom Burt, Larry Cohen, Sanjay Sidhu, Rainer Kuehling, Jim Foster, Sam Medici, Dan McCurdy, Dick Gerstner, David Jones, Marti Murphy, Kathryn Foreman, Katie Carter, Georgia Barnes, and of course the amazingly resourceful Joyce Schnepp.

Additional thanks go to Masanobu Katoh of Fujitsu; Ruud Peters at Philips; Yoshihide Nakamura of Sony; Editor Joff Wild at *Intellectual Asset Management* magazine; Senior Associate Vice President for Development David Kennedy at Stanford University; and Professors Wesley Cowen and Ashish Arora at Duke University, Naomi Lamoreaux at UCLA, Iain Cockburn of Boston University, and Bo Heiden at Stockholm University.

We wish also to express our special gratitude to our editor at John Wiley & Sons, Susan McDermott, for her enthusiasm and insight; to our rock of an agent, the ever-supportive and highly prolific Jim Levine at the Levine/Greenberg Agency; to our friend and colleague Dan Burstein, for his perspective and wisdom about book writing and publishing; and to our tireless and masterful editorial assistant, Jennifer Powell.

Finally, as anyone who has ever written a book knows, it is the author's family who bears a special burden in such an endeavor and deserves special recognition. We offer this now, with all our love and gratitude, to both our families.

Introduction

Why should anyone care what happens at Microsoft? This was the first question my coauthor David Kline and I asked ourselves when we sat down to consider writing this book in the summer of 2007. Thankfully, among all the questions that we would face over the next year and a half, this one was the easiest to answer.

New technology, after all, is the beating heart of innovation and global economic growth. So when arguably the most powerful technology company on earth engineers a radical 180-degree change in its business strategy and practices—abandoning its single-minded strategy of go-it-alone market conquest in favor of industry collaboration, and opening up its vast technological treasure chest to other companies and individuals—it's hardly surprising that this transformation should have effects far beyond the company itself.

Although Microsoft employs only 95,000 people directly, its influence stretches much deeper into the global economy. Nearly half of the 35 million people employed in the worldwide information technology (IT) sector depend upon Microsoft software or related services for their jobs. This includes 42 percent of information technology employment in the United States, 47 percent of Irish IT employment, and 44 percent of IT employment in Malaysia. And for every dollar of revenue that Microsoft earns, other companies in the global Microsoft "ecosystem" generate $7.79 for themselves. In 2007, in fact, they earned a staggering $400 billion from Microsoft-related products and services, and invested close to $100 billion in their local economies.

Given its huge footprint in the global economy, therefore, it's no wonder that the recent goings-on at Microsoft should be the subject of speculation and debate among technologists, industry executives, regulators and policy makers, and of course the media.

Are the company's new joint product development and other collaborative relationships with other firms boosting competition in the industry, spurring the rate of innovation, and speeding time to market for new products and services? Are the company's new technology-sharing initiatives with local entrepreneurs all over the globe fueling the growth of national industries and economies? How was such an entrenched enterprise as Microsoft able to refashion its culture and business strategy in only a few years—and are there lessons here for others?

In one sense, though, all these questions can be distilled down to three key issues: For industry executives, has Microsoft become a good partner? For policy makers and antitrust regulators in the United States, Europe, and Japan, has this once-adjudicated monopolist become a good citizen? And for customers, is Microsoft's new technical collaboration efforts with other companies producing better products and services that more effectively meet their needs?

Ultimately, these questions will be answered by whether Microsoft continues to be a successful and profitable enterprise. But perhaps a tentative answer may already be deduced from the fact that during the past six years more than 500 companies large and small around the world have chosen to sign technology-sharing and collaboration agreements with Microsoft, nearly all remaining antitrust issues with regulators worldwide have now been resolved, and new partners and customers are streaming into the global Microsoft "ecosystem" in record numbers.

The reader will naturally ask why Microsoft embarked upon what one analyst has called "the biggest change it has undergone since it became a multinational company." Obviously, it was not because Microsoft had suddenly become some sort of high-tech Mother Teresa. To quote another analyst: "They're not pulling lepers out of the gutter."

No, the simple truth is that Microsoft was, is, and will forever remain an intensely competitive business whose primary goal is to make a profit for its shareholders by creating products and services that customers need. And it was for entirely *business* reasons that the company decided to change its approach.

Remember that at the start of this decade, Microsoft was on the defensive—beset on all sides by antitrust suits and costly litigation, and viewed by many in the technology industry as a monopolist and market bully. At the same time, the center of gravity of technology innovation was beginning to shift away from large corporate R&D centers to a more diverse array of companies, universities, and even individuals—with no company any longer able to accumulate by itself all the technologies and business competencies needed for success.

So how was Microsoft to survive and succeed in the emerging new era of "open innovation," where collaboration and co-operation between firms, rather than single-minded competitive warfare, would be the keystones of success?

This was the challenge facing Bill Gates and other senior executives at Microsoft, and they correctly determined that the company's old fortress mentality culture and go-it-alone market strategy were no longer suited to the emerging twenty-first-century business environment. A new culture and strategy would have to be created—one that relied to a much larger extent than ever before upon building mechanisms of collaboration with other firms so that Microsoft could add their technological strengths and market competencies to its own in order to achieve success.

Perhaps there is a parallel here in America's abandonment of its unilateralist go-it-alone foreign policy of recent years in favor of a more collaborative and mutualist approach better suited to the fragmented, disorderly, and multipolar world in which we live. While the recent inauguration of a new U.S. president certainly gave new hope to people all over the world, the United States will ultimately be judged by its behavior, not just its words. The same is true of Microsoft as well.

To be sure, it would be a mistake to overstate the role that intellectual property played in the changes at Microsoft, or imply that other factors such as innovation policy or trends in technology development were not also important. But intellectual property did serve as the primary and surprisingly-sturdy scaffolding upon which Microsoft was able to construct a whole set of new business practices and relations with others in the industry.

In the pages that follow, the reader will gain extraordinary behind-the-scenes access to the dramatic struggle within Microsoft to find a new direction—to the high-level deliberations of the company's senior-most executives, to the internal debates and conflicts among executives and rank-and-file employees alike over the company's new collaborative direction, and to the company's controversial top-secret partnership-building efforts with major open source companies and others around the world. Nothing was held back from this book save for information specifically prohibited from disclosure by confidentiality agreements that Microsoft signed with other companies. Indeed, the degree of access to Microsoft's inner workings granted to us—and the honest self-criticism offered by Microsoft leaders and employees alike—was unprecedented in the company's 34-year history.

But this is no authorized corporate biography. Microsoft paid not a penny for the writing or production of this book, nor did the company control the final content in any way. In fact, senior executives went out of their way to provide us with the information we requested.

Still, full disclosure by the authors is required. I am at this writing still a corporate officer of Microsoft, for which I obviously receive a salary. My coauthor David Kline, a noted journalist, author of the best-selling *Rembrandts in the Attic*, and an intellectual property consultant to a number of high-profile firms, has also worked for Microsoft. So we obviously cannot claim to have never benefited by our dealings with the company.

That said, I defy anyone to find a more honest and revealing book about Microsoft's inner workings—including its past mistakes and continuing challenges—than this one.

The book itself is the product of an unusually-symbiotic collaboration between the authors. For my part, I brought to the project the business and IP leadership experience of a 28-year career at IBM, as well as the lessons learned from my work in international business, public policy, and venture capital. David

Kline contributed not only his deep knowledge of intellectual property's dynamic role in business and the economy and his practical experience as an intellectual property consultant, but also his rare—indeed, unique—talent for demystifying complex IP issues and explaining them in a clear and relevant manner to a broad business audience. Many of the most important insights in this book are his, and I am grateful for his collaboration.

If there are lessons in this book for executives in every industry, we hope the one most taken to heart by readers is the role that intellectual property can play in liberating previously untapped value in a company and opening up powerful new business opportunities. Intellectual property is not just for the technologist or lawyer anymore, nor even simply an asset of high-tech companies alone. Now accounting for up to 80 percent of the market value of all publicly traded companies in the world, IP ought rightfully to command the interest and attention of all serious business leaders today. It is, after all, the single greatest wealth-creating asset of the modern corporation.

As you will see, IP is also an exquisitely-effective tool for fashioning market-winning partnerships with other firms—and, in Microsoft's own case, for sculpting an entirely new corporate culture and business strategy.

—Marshall Phelps
January 2009

Chapter 1

The Collaboration Imperative

O n Sunday, May 25, 2003, I was playing golf near my home in New Canaan, Connecticut, when I received an unexpected phone call.

"Hi, Marshall, this is Bill Gates," said the caller. "I know that Brad [Smith, Microsoft's general counsel] spoke with you yesterday about the offer. But I just wanted to reinforce our hope that you'll come to Microsoft and help us with this really big challenge that we're facing."

Bill and Brad had already outlined the nature of that challenge when I met with both of them nine days earlier at the company's Redmond, Washington, headquarters: a limited patent portfolio that failed to protect Microsoft's huge R&D investment or provide it with the new business opportunities created by today's fast-changing technology environment. In short, they said, Microsoft needed a first-class patenting program and an intellectual property (IP) strategy that could facilitate the close collaboration with other firms that Microsoft needed to succeed in this new landscape of business competition.

"I know you're enjoying your retirement now," Bill went on. "But I really believe you're the person with the right background to handle this job."

I told him that I'd have to talk to my wife first, but that the opportunity did indeed sound exciting.

"That would be great," Bill replied. "We're all familiar with the great work you did at IBM, and I'm really looking forward to working with you."

It appeared that Bill had read some of the press reports on my work at IBM, which noted how (to quote one report) I had "put IP on the corporate map and made senior management and Wall Street sit up and take notice of IP as a revenue generator." During my 28-year career at IBM, I had led the transformation of the company's patent licensing program into an almost $2 billion per year profit machine—more profit just from IP licensing, it should be noted, than the total earnings of all but the top 40 largest companies in America at the time. As one of the first senior executives in corporate America to see profit and competitive advantage where others had seen only legal documents sitting in the filing cabinets of corporate law departments, I had helped to kick-start a revolution in the way that companies manage their intellectual property portfolios.

Three days after the phone call, I met with Bill and Brad again. And over the course of several more days of discussion, we reached agreement on the scope of my responsibilities and the company's commitment to this effort. On June 5, 2003, Microsoft announced that I would become the company's corporate vice president of intellectual property.

The announcement had a rather electrifying effect. As one IP trade journal put it, "When the world's richest man hires the architect of the world's most lucrative intellectual property program, the [business world] takes notice." And when the world's richest man happens to also be regarded in some circles as the world's biggest monopolist, it's no wonder that his hiring of a high-profile patent "warrior" might have caused some alarm.

"The fact that Microsoft hired Marshall Phelps tells you everything you need to know about their intentions," insisted analyst Russell Parr in an interview with MSNBC at the time. According to Parr, I had been brought to Redmond to recreate the massive $2 billion-a-year IP royalty stream I had built for IBM in the 1990s.

Another cutthroat motive was suggested by the technology and business magazine *ZDNet*: "Microsoft is very keen to [use patents to] rein in Open Source," it argued, referring to the free software movement. "Marshall Phelps will do that."

Not for the first time, of course, the pundits were wrong. The idea that a significant industry force such as the open source movement could ever be hemmed in by me or anyone else was patently absurd. And in point of fact, a key objective of the licensing program we planned to launch was to build a cooperative bridge to the open source world in order to meet customer demands for greater interoperability between Windows and Linux software.

As for trying to recreate IBM's $2 billion-a-year IP royalty stream, suffice it to say that for a company that generates a billion dollars in free cash flow every month, a mindless focus on maximizing licensing income made no business sense at all. In all my talks with Bill and Brad, both before and after I was hired, we never once discussed the idea of building an IBM-style revenue juggernaut from patent licensing. Instead, we merely hoped that licensing might generate sufficient revenue to cover some or all of the costs of maintaining the patent portfolio.

What none of these nervous analysts seemed to realize was that my hiring had come at a moment of profound change for the company. For years, Microsoft had been on the defensive, beset on all sides by antitrust suits and costly litigation, and viewed by many in the technology industry as a monopolist and market bully. At the same time, the dynamics of technology development and the software business had begun to change radically, requiring Microsoft to adapt to the emerging era of "open innovation," in which collaboration between firms, rather than go-it-alone market conquest, would be the keystone of success.

Underlying Microsoft's desire for change was its recognition that technology development had become too widely dispersed and heterogeneous, the pace of innovation too rapid, and the competition for markets and customers too multifaceted and demanding for any one firm to go it alone anymore. Indeed, it was becoming increasingly difficult for even the largest companies to hold all the pieces of even their own product technology in their own hands anymore. This was true even for Microsoft, which invested billions of dollars a year in research and development. In this new, decentralized technology environment, therefore, companies like Microsoft would simply have to collaborate if they wanted to succeed.

Bill, Brad, and I were hardly the only ones who had come to this conclusion. Indeed, in an era in which inventions were building upon each other with such rapidity as to quickly render obsolete even the most far-sighted company's product development strategy, it was becoming clear to a growing number of business leaders that the only way to stay above the rushing waters of creative destruction was to stand on the firmament of alliances with other firms. Whereas some 80 percent of major innovations during the 1970s had come from inside a single company's own R&D labs, by the dawn of the twenty-first century, studies now showed, more than two-thirds of major new innovations involved some sort of interorganizational collaboration—either between private firms, or between firms and federal laboratories or research universities. Recognizing that fact, 7 out of 10 senior executives surveyed by *The Economist* would conclude that their best strategy for accelerating innovation was to increase collaboration with other firms.

As my colleague Masanobu Katoh, then-corporate vice president for intellectual property at the Japanese giant Fujitsu, recently noted: "We are a $45 billion company. We are into consumer products, computers, consulting, and services, even manufacturing. We do it all. But alas, doing it all is no longer enough. We can no longer succeed unless we collaborate with other companies."

This new "collaboration imperative," as I called it, was reshaping business and redefining the sources of competitive advantage. And more to the point, it was rewriting the rules that businesses have always followed for how they leverage and deploy intellectual property.

First and foremost, it meant that intellectual property could no longer be viewed solely as a *negative* right—meaning, the right to either prevent someone from using your technology and competing in your market, or to tax them in the form of licensing fees for the right to do so. From now on, IP's greatest value would lie not so much in being a weapon *against* competitors, but rather in serving as a *bridge to collaboration* with other firms that would enable companies to acquire the technologies and competencies they needed to compete successfully.

Indeed, intellectual property was becoming the sine qua non of open innovation itself. It provided the legal scaffolding upon which firms could share their most innovative research and partner together to create new products and services. Without IP rights, firms would resist sharing their ideas for fear that others would misappropriate their innovations. But with such rights, firms could share their innovations with others, secure in the knowledge that all were fully protected in deploying them to mutual advantage. Just as good fences made good neighbors, strong IP rights would make for strong and successful collaborations. And in the case of intellectual property, this so-called "fence" would turn out to be more of a bridge than a barrier between firms.

We Need Relationships

This was the vision that informed Microsoft's new direction. Because collaboration now appeared to be the key to Microsoft's future success, the company's greatest need was to start building relationships with other firms—large firms, small firms, open source firms, venture capitalists, software developers, even independent inventors. In short, Microsoft needed relationships with anyone and everyone it could find in order to remain at the center of technology innovation and at the forefront of new markets and business opportunities. And intellectual property was quite simply the best available vehicle for constructing those collaborative relationships. As the legal embodiment of any company's most precious resource—its innovation—Microsoft's IP defined the arena of cooperation and established clear rights and obligations for both sides in any joint endeavor.

Commenting on my hiring, the industry trade journal *eWeek* noted that "Gates agreed with Phelps that Microsoft was at an inflexion point in its history" and needed to cooperate more with other firms. *Newsweek* magazine, meanwhile, reported that

I took the job "only after Gates promised [me] he wanted to change the way Microsoft interfaced with the technology world."

It's important to recognize that my hiring was only the latest in a whole series of moves on the part of Microsoft's senior leaders to repair the company's relations with the industry and government. A year earlier Bill Gates and CEO Steve Ballmer had appointed Brad Smith as the firm's new general counsel, based, in part, upon Smith's insistence that "it was time to make peace" and establish more mutually beneficial relations with other companies. And Smith had already moved swiftly to translate that vision of peace and collaboration into reality by resolving dozens of legal cases against the company, including Microsoft's 2002 antitrust settlement with states' attorneys general, its data privacy agreements with the Federal Trade Commission and the European authorities, and, later on, antitrust and intellectual property disputes with AOL Time Warner, Sun Microsystems, RealNetworks, IBM, and Novell.

As Ballmer told *BusinessWeek:* "The company has made it a priority to do all we can to end these legal issues and to do so in a way that increases collaboration with other companies."

The company's efforts in this regard were profoundly important in setting the stage internally for Microsoft's new intellectual property and technology initiatives, even before my arrival. As Brad Smith would later tell a Harvard University forum commemorating the tenth anniversary of the U.S. Justice Department's antitrust suit against Microsoft, "Part of our maturation process really required that we start to see ourselves the way other people were seeing us. It was not necessarily an easy thing to do. It seldom is when you go through that kind of process. But it spurred us to take a more principled approach. It enabled us to do business in a different way. And I think it has served us and the industry well."

I must confess that I was humbled by the prospect of helping such a powerful high-tech leader to develop a new vision for the collaborative use of intellectual property in the age of open innovation. Microsoft is a company, after all, with an enormous footprint in the global information technology industry—a high-tech Bigfoot if ever there was one.

Microsoft itself employs 95,000 people worldwide. But consider that of the 35 million people employed worldwide as of 2007 in the $1.2-trillion-a-year information technology (IT) sector, an astonishing 42 percent—or 14.7 million people—are employed either directly by Microsoft or by firms that make products that run on Microsoft software, provide support for Microsoft software, or otherwise participate in the global Microsoft "ecosystem." This includes 181,200 Microsoft-based jobs in Malaysia (44 percent of Malaysia's IT ecosystem), 71,607 Microsoft-related jobs in Ireland (47 percent of Ireland's IT workforce), and 4.2 million Microsoft-related jobs in the United States (42 percent of our domestic IT workforce).

What's more, the 640,000 vendors in this global Microsoft ecosystem earned more than $425 billion in revenue in 2007, invested close to $100 billion in local national economies, and their employees paid more than $514 billion ($203 billion in the United States alone) in taxes that year.

In short, Microsoft is a vital engine of the global economy. And if it were going to embark on a new initiative to share its technology and intellectual property with any and all interested firms—including competitors—and launch technical and market collaborations with both the largest multinational enterprises as well as the smallest startups and entrepreneurs, this could not help but have profound effects on the shape and direction of the whole technology industry. What's more, I was acutely aware that our efforts to adapt to the new "collaboration imperative" would inevitably offer lessons—both positive and negative—not only for IP managers but for senior executives throughout the information technology sector as well.

But to understand where Microsoft needed to go, it was necessary to first appreciate where it had been—and why, in the view of many inside and outside the company, the company had developed a "fortress mentality" towards its technology that it now needed to overcome.

A Lesson in Patent Holdups

One of the most insightful historians of Microsoft's development is Nathan Myhrvold, Microsoft's chief technology officer (CTO) from 1986 to 1999, and later the founder of the invention and intellectual property licensing firm Intellectual Ventures. A brilliant mathematician, amateur archeologist, and world-class photographer, Myhrvold has an uncensored ebullience that comes partly from his personality, and partly from being a billionaire.

"When I first came to Microsoft in 1986, patents meant nothing to the company," recalls Myhrvold. "I think they had two patent applications, but most people didn't even know what the word 'patent' meant. For one thing, software wasn't widely understood to be patentable back then. And within the software industry as a whole, there wasn't any focus on it. We were still just trying to legitimize the notion that software itself was a real business apart from hardware."

(Actually, the legal basis for patenting software was established in the 1981 Supreme Court decision *Diamond v. Diehr*, which affirmed that software and computer-implemented inventions could be patented. Software patenting didn't become widespread until the Federal Circuit Court's *Allapat* decision in 1995, which led the U.S. Patent and Trademark (PTO) office to issue Examination Guidelines for Computer-Related Inventions a year later.)

"But over time," Myhrvold adds, "I began to realize the importance of doing more advanced research and development, and of securing patents for our discoveries so we could control our own technological destiny. In 1991, we finally founded Microsoft Research, which is now the largest private research organization in the world—bigger even than Pfizer's, Merck's, or even IBM's research arm. And we started filing more patents."

But Myhrvold soon realized just how deep Microsoft's patent deficit actually was. "As Microsoft got bigger," he explains, "all sorts of companies started coming around to see us. They'd claim that we were infringing their patents, and demand that we take a license. And I was like, 'Oh my God, they can do this? They can just demand money from us?' A lot of people were shocked by that, I can tell you. And when our lawyers looked around and asked what sort of patents we could assert back against these companies—in a sort of 'mutual assured destruction' show-down that would enable us to cross-license without having to fork over a lot of money—the answer was, 'We don't have crap.' So every time one of these companies came by to assert their patents against us, it would cost us money. Sometimes 50 or 100 million dollars. And that's a lot of zeroes to give away just because someone else has patents and you don't."

At times the patent gold digging took on comic overtones. "There was this one guy named Efraim Arazi, who started a pioneering computer graphics company called Electronics for Imaging, or EFI for short," recalls Myhrvold. "This also happened to be his nickname—Efi—so obviously this was a guy with no small ego. But that's true of a lot of geniuses, and Efi was a genius. He was a founder or cofounder of several companies, and an outstanding engineer. But his most brilliant idea was to license this seminal patent from MIT that was the result of eight years and $4 million worth of research into color imaging and printing technology. A total of four Ph.D. and 12 masters degrees were awarded to researchers who contributed to that project. And Efi licensed the patent that resulted from all this work for only $25,000, plus royalties."

Myhrvold smiles at the memory. "So Efi takes this patent and starts making the rounds. He shows up at Kodak about one week after that famous Polaroid judgment [in which Kodak was ordered to pay Polaroid $925 million for patent infringement, the largest patent award in U.S. history at the time]. And in that inimitable style of his, he says—and here you have to imagine his Israeli accent—'So, Kodak, you're not doing so well, eh? Well, look at this patent I have here.' And Kodak says, 'Oh God, not again!' and immediately writes him a check for $10 million. Then he goes to Adobe with this same patent and makes them an offer they can't refuse, either. So that's another $10 million. And finally he comes to Microsoft."

Myhrvold laughs at the memory of Arazi's audacity. "So Efi and I sit down in a room with our patent attorney, and he starts telling us the story of the $20 million he's already gotten for his little $25,000 patent and how the money is funding his new company. 'Hey, this is better than getting money from venture capitalists,' he gushes. 'I don't even have to give up any equity!'

"And then all of a sudden," adds Myhrvold, "Efi turns to our patent attorney and says, 'So, Mister Patent Attorney, did you know Windows is infringing my patent?'

"Well, our patent attorney, who was this very buttoned-down guy, suddenly doesn't look so well," Myhrvold explains, "so he leaves the room to go to the bathroom. As soon as he's

11

out of the room, Efi starts in on him. 'Oh my God, he's going to go home, he's going to go slap his wife and yell at her for buying him that stupid tie!' And I can't help myself. I'm laughing my head off. I mean, Efi really was a character."

But after sharing a good laugh, Myhrvold says he got serious. "I sort of cleared my throat and told Efi very firmly that unlike Kodak and Adobe, we didn't have color management. So he could go pound sand as far as I was concerned."

Efi's response? "'Okay,' Efi said, 'no problem.' He was like, 'Hey, it was worth a try!'"

But perhaps the most painful lesson in Microsoft's early patent education was delivered by a small company named Stac Electronics. Explains Myhrvold: "Stac had a disk compression program for our old DOS operating system called Stacker. And in 1991, I think it was, we started negotiating with Stac to see if we could license their compression program and integrate it into the new 6.0 version of DOS we were about to release. Well, we couldn't reach a deal—I don't remember what the problem was—so instead we simply decided to design around Stac's patent. Sure, it cost us more money to design our own compression tool, which we called DoubleSpace, than if we had just licensed it from Stac. But since we couldn't get the license, we had no choice."

Insists Myhrvold: "We really did design around their patent. We came up with a whole new way to achieve disk compression that was different from the way they did it. Stacker used X, Y, and Z methods to achieve compression, whereas our compression program used P, Q, and R methods to get a similar result. Which is exactly what we're supposed to do under patent law. We believed it was perfectly legal. We felt very confident that we didn't infringe their patent, and that we could prove it. So, we figured, game over."

Except that the game was not over. "When we released DOS 6.0 with that DoubleSpace feature, they sued us for infringing their patent anyway," Myhrvold recalls. "Not only that, but while we were working to design around their patent, Stac had gone out and bought this old data compression patent owned by Ferranti International Signal, a British aerospace contractor, which had developed it for a satellite system. It was originally filed as a hardware patent—this was before software patents were even allowed—but the claims were written broadly enough that a court could interpret it to apply to software as well. Stac paid a quarter of a million dollars to buy that little patent. And they bought it specifically to use against us."

Myhrvold sighs ruefully. "I was totally shocked. I remember asking our attorneys, 'They can do this? They can just go buy a patent and then use it retroactively against us?' And they said 'Yep.' And I remember, I just went, 'Aw, hell . . .'"

He shrugs. "So Stac won a judgment against us for $120 million. The jury said we infringed. We appealed, but later settled with them for something like a $40 million investment in their company and an additional $43 million in royalties. All because of a patent they bought for a quarter million dollars."

It would later turn out, of course, that Stac's patent purchase was merely a harbinger of the sort of wholesale purchasing of patent rights for assertion against deep-pocketed firms that we see everywhere today. This can be an especially egregious practice, bordering on extortion, when committed by firms that don't produce any products—the infamous "patent trolls."

"We were driving over patent landmines every day," Myhrvold remembers. "It was terrible. And it wasn't just us. The whole software industry paid no attention to patents in those days. You know, back then we were all just hell-bent on shipping product next week. So the Stac suit really drove it home to me that Microsoft was in real danger on the patent front. It was a major lesson to me."

And for Bill Gates as well. Indeed, it was precisely in response to the ever-growing number of patent holdups by firms such as Stac that Microsoft after 1993 began requiring all its partners and OEMs to agree to a non-assertion of patents (NAP) clause in their deals. The NAP clause would later prove to be a major bone of contention between Microsoft and the industry—and its abandonment ten years later by Microsoft would likewise prove to be the key factor in enabling the company to forge a new and healthier relationship with the industry—but it's important to understand the defensive origins of Microsoft's "fortress mentality" practices.

In the words of Horacio Gutierrez, who in 2006 would succeed me as vice president of intellectual property and licensing at Microsoft, "You have to remember what it was like for this company in those days. We were this odd group of people competing against the biggest forces in the high-tech world to create this new software industry. It was not necessarily obvious at that time that software was a viable business apart from hardware. And when you're fighting for your survival like that, you have a tendency to be protective—especially if you're a start-up in a new emerging business sector. It was only later, as we matured, that we began to realize—and our customers began to tell us—that we didn't need to be so defensive anymore and that, with our growth, we had to assume a larger responsibility for the health of the whole industry."

In fact, it is precisely Microsoft's ability to change that impresses Gutierrez most about the company: "The only constant that you find in the history of this company is this almost relentless willingness to re-examine ourselves," he insists. "That, and a willingness to reinvent ourselves and shed the things that are preventing us from moving forward."

In any event, these patent holdups eventually got Myhrvold thinking about Microsoft's future as well as his own. "I realized that patents were becoming incredibly valuable in today's world, and they were going to be vital to any company that wanted to control its own technological destiny." So convinced was he of the importance and value of patents—not only to business, but to America's innovative capacity and competitiveness as well—that he eventually resigned from Microsoft in 1999 and started his own firm, Intellectual Ventures (IV), to invest in invention and the development of a liquid market for patents.

This is how I came to know Myhrvold—by becoming an early partner in Intellectual Ventures as well as IV's negotiator with Microsoft on its 2003 investment in the IV invention fund. One week I sat on IV's side of the table, discussing investment terms with Microsoft negotiators John Weresh, a leading IP attorney, and Kenneth Lustig, one of the company's top dealmakers and strategists in the corporate development group. The next week, after agreeing to take the Microsoft job, I was on the Microsoft side of the table, as Weresh and Lustig's boss.

In fact, the very day I started at Microsoft, Bill and Brad directed Weresh and Lustig to go ahead and get the IV investment closed and obtain the best possible terms for Microsoft, which they did. The IV investment was very important to Microsoft, given the increasing numbers of patent suits it faced as well as the company's paramount interest in seeking opportunities to collaborate with others. According to Lustig, "We began to realize during the course of our negotiations with IV that there were some very positive opportunities that could be realized by embracing IP as a business in a thorough and cross-functional way. Critical to realizing these opportunities would be the building of wide-ranging IP relationships in the industry, with both partners and competitors alike, to reduce litigation conflicts and work toward a common set of interests."

In any event, shifting from one side of the table to the other left me with an odd feeling—rather like some sort of hemispherical brain malfunction. And it made me realize yet again how small the world really is.

Small, perhaps, but no less challenging for the intimacy of my connections. My job was to reform and invigorate Microsoft's IP department, which in my view had been functioning like a football team composed only of defensive linemen, with no one knowing how to throw a forward pass. To be sure, there were people in other corporate groups within Microsoft who were trying to play offense and build partnerships, but these efforts were not broad enough. And no one was yet systematically looking for ways to employ the company's intellectual property as the glue for cementing sturdy partnerships with other firms.

This would have to change. I knew that we had to develop an intellectual property strategy that could help the company achieve its most critical business objectives. These were to transform Microsoft's relations with the industry so that we could better participate in the new and more distributed environment for technology innovation, pursue joint development efforts with other companies, gain access to technology we needed, and pursue joint marketing and sales opportunities wherever possible. But how exactly to do all of this, I wasn't quite sure.

Which, come to think of it, is exactly the same spot I was in just a decade earlier.

It's Déjà vu All over Again

In hindsight, it's now clear that my rather eclectic series of jobs at IBM was leading me inexorably towards the use of intellectual property as a financial and strategic asset in IBM's recovery from its near-death experience. But at the time, I could see no clear pattern in my dissatisfied wanderings through the IBM bureaucracy. All I knew was that I wanted to do something that combined legal and business activity. But what that was, I had no idea.

I started out in the legal department in 1970 and held a variety of positions there. But I was never totally sold on staying within legal. For one thing, IBM's legal department had a reputation as an organizational black hole—a "roach motel" that let you check in but not check out. So I was thrilled when, after some major antitrust litigation that I worked on came to a close, my bosses decided to send me to Stanford business school. The company paid all the bills—my apartment, telephone, nursery school for the kids, my salary, the whole bit. It was a great gig.

When I graduated from business school in 1980, I went to work for the then–chairman of the company, Frank Cary. Now, in IBM's universe, becoming an assistant to the chairman or president was considered the best training with an eye towards the future. You studied at the feet of the master, so to speak, working on whatever projects he happened to be focused on. It was considered a springboard to a higher management career.

Over the next 13 months, I worked very closely with both Cary and IBM's general counsel—the former U.S. attorney general and undersecretary of state under President Johnson, Nicholas deB. Katzenbach—on two key issues: how to settle the Justice Department antitrust suit against IBM, and what the future organization of IBM should look like, beyond the issues that could arise if we lost the antitrust suit. We already had two plans—a Red Plan and a Blue Plan—for splitting IBM into two different companies if we lost the suit. Our work focused on how we could rationalize the company if we won or otherwise settled the antitrust suit and remained a single enterprise. At the time, IBM was plagued with a duplication of structures and efforts. These parallel universes were developed to protect IBM if the company was ever broken up. As a result, we had laboratories and plants whose main competitors were other IBM laboratories and plants.

It was a great learning experience for me. We visited various IBM laboratories and factories all over the world, trying to figure out whether we had the right structures and the right divisions in place. I didn't realize it at the time, but this experience would prove to be enormously helpful to me later on.

After that, I held various legal positions over the next few years—including general counsel for the personal computer business at IBM and managing attorney for the law department—but again, I had the education and the training and most of all the desire to do something more, something in the business arena. Finally, in 1984, I was asked to help lead the company's Asia business as vice president of IBM's Asia/Pacific Group.

My new assignment to Japan was actually part of a major corporate restructuring in which IBM hived off a piece of its corporate headquarters and sent it to Asia. The reason for this was really quite simple, although younger executives may find it hard to understand nowadays. Recall that this happened before the Internet and even before the widespread use of faxes, at a time when it might take all night for a teletype machine to crank out a few pages of a document. As a result, we found it was very difficult to run a business that stretched from India in the west, to Japan in the east, to Korea in the north, and then all the way south to New Zealand—all from corporate headquarters in Armonk, New York. We were constantly putting people on airplanes and flying them back to headquarters to discuss what sort of bids we were going to make for various pieces of the Asia mainframe business. And we discovered that, as often as not, by the time the bid details were worked out and the negotiators flew back to the Far East, we had lost the deal.

So we needed a new way to run the Asia business. And in typical IBM fashion, we did it juggernaut style. We moved 500 families to Japan, something no other American corporation had ever done. One of the Japanese newspapers called it "McArthur's Second Invasion."

"You're Stealing Our Software!"

At about the same time as my posting to Tokyo, IBM began to suspect that the Japanese manufacturers who built clones of our mainframe computers—Hitachi, Mitsubishi, and Fujitsu being the three biggest ones—were illegally copying our mainframe software.

According to the consent decree IBM signed with the U.S. Justice Department in 1956, we were required to license our intellectual property to everyone in the world on reasonable and non-discriminatory terms. But after 1969, when we unbundled our software from the hardware and sold it separately, it was our view that Japanese mainframe manufacturers needed to create their own software for these machines. Yet despite being relative newcomers to mainframe software, their software somehow managed to accurately match the capabilities of our own.

So we commissioned some of our top programming and security experts to do some detailed forensic work on the Japanese software. That's when our suspicions quickly gave way to certainty. Apparently, one of the programmers in Poughkeepsie, New York, who had designed the IBM software, named one of the loops in the program after his girlfriend, whose name, if I recall, was Judy. And our forensics revealed that the same name—"Judy"—appeared in the source code of the Japanese software. Now Judy is not a very common name in Japan, so this turned out to be the silver bullet that proved the Japanese had infringed our software intellectual property.

We brought the matter up with Fujitsu, Mitsubishi, and Hitachi, and the latter two firms settled rather quickly. But negotiations with Fujitsu were another matter entirely. On the IBM side we had Ralph Pfieffer, the head of IBM World Trade, and John Opal, who would later serve as IBM's CEO. Vice Chairman Michio Naruto led the Fujitsu team. We would meet in a suite at one of the major hotels—usually the Okura, because it was centrally located—and the negotiations quickly became very difficult, and very personal, as well. These were not civil discussions at all. I recall one incident in which the two sides literally screamed at each other from across the room.

"Fujitsu is acting immorally," Ralph Pfeiffer charged. "You're stealing our software!"

Vice Chairman Naruto bolted out of his seat: "You Americans are just trying to keep Japan down! You don't like it that you are no longer the masters in our relationship."

It's important to understand some of the geopolitical dynamics that were contributing to the animosity in that room, for it was not simply these two companies, Fujitsu and IBM, who were responsible for the hard feelings. The 1980s were a very difficult period in U.S.-Japan relations. Japanese industrial and financial power was clearly ascendant, whereas the United States had lost much of its competitive edge, not only in consumer electronics but in a number of manufacturing sectors as well. To put it bluntly, Japan was beating the crap out of America in a variety of competitive arenas. And we were scared.

In any event, after years of negotiations and arbitration, Fujitsu finally settled under terms similar to those agreed to by Hitachi and Mitsubishi. A substantial sum of money was involved that was nonetheless smaller than the amount they would have had to pay to develop their own software. And today, ironically, not only does IBM cooperate with Fujitsu in a variety of endeavors, but I am also proud to call Naruto-san, now retired as vice chairman of Fujitsu, a very good friend. Whenever I am back in Tokyo, we get together and laugh about old times.

I learned many things during that trying time in Japan. I developed a deeper appreciation for the diversity of human experience and the importance of trying to see the world through other-than-American eyes. But even more important, I received my very first lesson in the enormous value and importance of intellectual property to corporate, and indeed national, success—especially as it related to software technology.

I carried this lesson back home with me when in 1987 I was appointed IBM's director of governmental programs in Washington, D.C. This was a public policy job in which my task was to promote government and industry cooperation to enhance technology innovation and the competitiveness of U.S. industry around the world. I had seen how Japanese industry and government cooperated to strengthen that country's competitive posture in the world. And we looked for ways that we might be able to achieve some of the same result, albeit in a way that better suited our own nation's more laissez faire economic system.

During this time, we helped form the Council on Competitiveness, which played a crucial role in spotlighting issues of national competitiveness and innovation for both government and industry policymakers. Along with my counterparts at Hewlett-Packard, Sun, and other firms, I helped organize the first "CEO Forum" in 1989 under the auspices of the Computer Systems Policy Project, which brought the top people from the dozen largest computer makers (the "hardware guys") together for the first time. These people were not used to working together, or indeed even talking to each other, on matters of joint concern, so we didn't know how the event would turn out. In fact, I was quoted in *BusinessWeek* as saying, "We weren't sure these guys could have dinner together without getting into a food fight." But in the end, it was successful in not only establishing ties between America's high-tech CEOs that have persisted to this day, but also in lobbying Washington to regulate Japanese trade and dumping practices.

Again, you have to remember that this was a time of great concern in the United States about the state of American industry. The number of new inventions being patented by U.S. technology companies was in rapid decline. Even IBM, which had previously been a leading U.S. patentee, was in danger of falling off the top-ten patenting chart completely, as were other great American companies such as General Electric. In contrast, Japanese companies such as Fujitsu, Mitsubishi, and Hitachi had soared to the top of the patenting and innovation chart.

The bottom line was that we once thought we had the information technology world to ourselves, only to discover that our king-of-the-mountain position on the high-tech landscape was being cratered by the Japanese. And looming on the horizon were the Taiwanese and the Koreans.

In retrospect, of course, it's now clear that we failed to appreciate both the vitality and resilience of U.S. innovation as well as the thin reed that the Japanese model of competitiveness, with its tight industry-government cooperation, was really built upon. We also didn't realize the extent to which that Japanese industrial juggernaut was fueled by a huge real estate and financial bubble that would ultimately collapse by the end of the 1990s.

In any event, after four years in Washington, I was ready to move on. It wasn't because I thought my policy work around competitiveness wasn't important. Rather, it's that I'm basically apolitical—I'm neither a Democrat nor a Republican—and it seems to me if you're going to be in a political position like that, you ought to know if you're a boy or a girl, so to speak.

So when IBM's then-chairman, John Akers, came to Washington in late 1991 to lobby government officials on some matter, he and I went to dinner and he offered me one of three corporate vice-presidencies. One choice was to stay where I was, only with additional responsibility as a corporate vice president. Another was vice president of finance for the PC business. And the third was vice president of commercial and industry relations, or C&IR. For reasons far too Byzantine to explain here, C&IR and not the law department was responsible for IBM's intellectual property portfolio, among other duties. I decided to take the C&IR job, where I felt I could put my growing interest in technology innovation and intellectual property to some use.

IBM on the Ropes

It turned out that I took over the intellectual property portfolio at a crucial time for IBM, because the company was literally on its deathbed. Over the next two years, IBM sustained $15.4 billion in losses—it lost $8.1 billion in 1992 alone, the largest corporate loss up to that point in U.S. business history—and sales of its old standby mainframes, from which 90 percent of the firm's profits were derived, had dropped by half. By the time John Akers retired and the board hired Lou Gerstner to take over as CEO in April of 1993, the company had fewer than 100 days of cash remaining in the bank.

The reasons for Big Blue's decline were varied, but taken together they pointed to a bureaucratic lack of innovation and an arrogant refusal to adjust to changing market conditions. The company had completely missed the minicomputer trend, was a laggard in the PC business, was losing mainframe market share hand over fist, and was saddled with a costly overhead that included all sorts of duplicative programs and a policy of lifetime employment that prevented IBM from weeding out under-performing managers. Instead of innovating, all we were doing was hemorrhaging red ink and propping up outmoded business models.

So the first thing I did as vice president of C&IR was to change its name to Intellectual Property and Licensing (IP&L) and shut down its industry relations and other programs. I laid off about half of my organization—probably close to a hundred people. Of course that was only a drop in the bucket compared to the retrenchment going on throughout the company at that time. Indeed, the layoffs and restructuring would eventually trim the IBM workforce to half its former size. We went from 407,000 employees in 1986 to barely 200,000 a decade later.

It's one thing to get rid of a deadwood operation, of course, and quite another to actually do something that positively enhances the company's business prospects. So I began to look closely at the economics of the company's R&D and its relationship to our patenting efforts. We were spending more and more every year on R&D, yet filing fewer and fewer patents to protect that R&D investment. So I decided that IBM was going to start patenting aggressively again. We set a goal of becoming number one on America's patenting chart. We made it by 1993, just a year and a half after I took over the IP function, and IBM has remained number one ever since.

Filing thousands of patents, of course, is not cheap. So I looked for ways to transform the economics of our effort so that it would become a profit center rather than a cost center for the company. I realized that licensing our intellectual property would bring in royalties from companies that used our technology, but I wasn't sure how much. One thing I was sure of, though, was that the only way to get IBM's divisions to go along with licensing technology to other firms, including competitors, was to share the proceeds with them. So I decided that every dollar of royalties that we brought in from licensing should go right back to the divisions.

Now, that was a very radical idea in American business at the time—not just sharing your technology with others, which was considered heresy in many quarters, but using the proceeds from such licensing to not only fund the patenting and licensing operations themselves but also to enhance the bottom line of the company's divisions. But I was able to get away with it for one simple reason—the old CEO, Akers, was on his way out, but the new CEO, Gerstner, was not yet fully in charge. I was able to do it because no one was there to stop me.

To make this licensing effort successful, however, I knew I had to find a partner among the divisions to help develop a proof of concept. So I went to see Mike Attardo, the chief of the microelectronics division, which was then going through a very rough time with the transition from bipolar to CMOS (complimentary metal oxide semiconductor) chip technology.

"Mike," I told him, "you're laying off all these bipolar engineers. Why not give me 10 of them—along with some scanning, tunneling microscopes so they can analyze the chips being made by our competitors? And I'll bet you I can make 25 million bucks for your division."

Now, this was a pretty attractive offer for a guy like Attardo, given that his division, like most at IBM at the time, was on the ropes financially. I mean, here's some guy offering him $25 million, for which he doesn't have to do a damn thing except lend some engineers and some microscopes? He said fine, no skin off his behind. And that first year we made him $48 million.

How did we do it? We used these scanning, tunneling microscopes, which can examine objects at the molecular level, to look at the chips made by our competitors. And lo and behold, we discovered that in a number of cases the grooves that were etched in competitors' chips—they're called "vias"—were exact, and I mean *exact*, replicas of the grooves used in IBM chips.

Now, it takes a very precise chemical process to etch chips in exactly the way that IBM had etched them. There's only one way to do it, in fact, and we had patented it. So we used these microscopes to photograph the vias in other companies' chips, and then we'd go meet with those companies and suggest that maybe they needed to take a license to our technology.

There we'd be, all of us sitting around a conference table—lawyers and engineers from both of our companies—and it was the same process in every meeting we held. We'd ask the other side to please explain to us how the vias in their chips could so perfectly match our own, down to the molecular level. Because, so far as we knew, there was only one way on earth to do it, and we had patented that method. And there would be an awkward silence from the other side.

Did anyone ever admit to infringing our patents? No, of course not. But a couple of weeks later, the other company would get back to us and agree that perhaps a license between our two companies would be a good idea after all. Eventually, they all took licenses.

Now, it should be noted that the licensing deals we signed were not confiscatory. Besides ensuring that other firms paid for our technology when they used it, we usually tried to license them additional technology or know-how so that they felt that they were getting a good deal. In fact, this licensing effort of ours was one of the first examples in American industry of companies licensing and sharing technology with other firms for mutual benefit.

What's more, while I ran the IP organization for IBM, I never sued anybody (and I take pride in the fact that I rarely sued when I later ran the IP organization at Microsoft). This is no small feat in an age when patent litigation has become a burden on business. Of course, sometimes you have to litigate when the other party has stolen your hard-earned innovation and refuses to resolve the problem. And even a non-litigious company like Microsoft has had to sue one or two companies in the past couple of years, but only as a last resort. But in general, I believe the world would be a lot better off if more companies would treat their intellectual property primarily as a business and financial asset and not a litigation club for beating damage awards out of rivals.

In any event, after our success with the licensing program in the microelectronics division, word started getting around to the various divisions that we could make real money for them. And given that we had already spent the money to do the underlying R&D, the revenues from licensing were 98 percent pure profit. So suddenly other divisions wanted to work with us to license their technology as well. This became a virtuous circle as the revenues raised became part of the following year's divisional business plans.

But while support for our program was growing, there was a lot of pushback as well. For one thing, the divisions tended to see the technology they developed as belonging to them, not to the whole company. And they viewed the whole notion of technology sharing as heresy. After all, throughout the entire history of American business, the goal had always been to keep your technology from your competitors. So licensing was viewed as a radical new idea.

There was also, as you would expect, a good deal of opposition from some of the companies we targeted for licensing. Those that were IBM mainframe customers would often respond by calling an IBM sales manager and complaining about the way they were being treated. Then that IBM sales manager would call me and scream about how I was screwing up their sales relationships with these firms. Sometimes both of them would complain directly to the CEO's office, which would then call me and demand an explanation.

Convincing the Big Boss

Most of these complaints I was able to beat back. But when I got a call from Lou Gerstner himself on perhaps the second or third day after he took command at IBM, I worried that perhaps the jig was finally up.

"What the hell are you doing?" he demanded.

"Er, um, what do you mean?" I replied.

"Are you licensing our technology to competitors?"

"Yes, I am," I told him.

"So then I ask you again," he sighed, obviously frustrated. "What the hell do you think you're doing? Why aren't you using our patents to stop our competitors in their tracks?"

There it was again—the idea that intellectual property was simply a weapon for blocking other companies rather than a financial asset and a vehicle for collaborating with other firms.

"Lou," I said, "let me come to your office and prove to you why it's a good idea."

"Fine," he said, "I'm eager to hear it."

I hung up the phone and turned to the two colleagues who were sitting in the office with me. "Now what?" I asked them. "How do we do this?"

So we started batting ideas around for how to make the case for licensing to Lou. I have to admit that I was more than a little nervous. After all, Lou Gerstner was an outsider—he had come from RJR Nabisco and American Express—and he had absolutely zero loyalty to anyone in the corporate bureaucracy who didn't pull his or her own weight. We had no doubt that he was going to fire every single corporate officer in IBM if that's what it took to get the company out of its doldrums (and, in fact, he eventually did fire almost every corporate officer in headquarters). So we couldn't bluff this one. We couldn't just use some pretty overlays with pie charts to convince him. We had to come up with something tangible, something real and undeniable, to demonstrate that our licensing program was vital to IBM's survival and recovery.

And then one of the guys—I forget exactly who—said, "Why not crack open a laptop and show him everything that we've licensed?" So that's what we did. We pried off the top of an IBM laptop, and the keyboard case as well, and then we glued a bunch of little map flags—toothpicks with red flags on them—to every single technological component in the computer that we had licensed from other companies. After a couple of hours, we had 150 of these little flags sticking out from almost every square inch of that laptop. And the only reason we stopped there is that we simply ran out of room. And bear in mind, this was IBM's own computer architecture—and yet IBM still needed the intellectual property of other firms to build it.

Later that afternoon, we brought the laptop to Lou's office. My memory of events is a bit sketchy after 16 years, but the gist of what happened is as follows:

"Take a look at that," I told him. "We can't even build our own computers without other people's technology. The whole technology world is interdependent now, and there's no going back. There's no way we're ever going to get out of the licensing game."

Lou was silent, still staring at that laptop with all those little red flags.

"So here's our idea, Lou," I continued. "If we have to license anyway just to stay in business, why not make some money from it?"

With less than a hundred days cash left in the company, of course, that got his attention.

He looked up at me. "How much money?" he asked.

I paused, took a deep breath and looked up at the ceiling. "A billion dollars," I said. "We'll make you a billion dollars by the end of this decade."

He looked at me very hard then. I could tell he was debating whether to ask me how I came up with that ridiculous billion-dollar number, but he decided to let it pass. Which was a lucky thing, because I had totally grabbed that number out of thin air. I suspect he probably guessed as much, but since no one else in the company was promising to make him a billion dollars, I suppose he decided what the hell, let this Phelps character go for it.

"What do you need?" he asked.

"Just leave me alone," I replied, "and I'll make you that billion dollars. But I've got to have the authority to do what I want with the IP. I can't have the business managers telling me it belongs to them and their divisions. And I can't have the sales managers complaining every time I try to get one of their big customers to take a license from us."

Lou nodded quietly, then said "Okay."

And sure enough, he later sent an e-mail to everyone in the company—it was probably his very first e-mail at IBM, if not the first e-mail he had ever sent in his life—informing them that the intellectual property of the various divisions belongs to the IBM corporation, not to the divisions. And that sole authority for its use belongs to the IP and Licensing group.

"Intellectual property assets such as patents belong to IBM, not to the individual units," Gerstner wrote. "It is one of our key corporate assets and must be protected. Negotiations concerning intellectual property with companies outside IBM are the responsibility of the Intellectual Property and Licensing staff."

In the end, we reached a billion dollars in cumulative licensing revenues—not in seven years as I had promised Lou, but in three years. In fact, we earned a phenomenal $1.9 billion in the year 2000 alone, which was when I retired from IBM. And 98 percent of that was pure profit—all except for the $36 million it cost me to run the department. Bottom line, our intellectual property-licensing program contributed 25 percent of IBM's total profit for that year.

IP Must Serve the Business

Many analysts and reporters have written about the success we achieved in building such a lucrative intellectual property-licensing program at IBM. But all too often, they have missed the real lesson from our success. They have talked about the IP licensing effort as a business in its own right, and this had the unfortunate effect of contributing to a mistaken belief on the part of some companies that they, too, could replicate IBM's billion-dollar IP revenue stream. Those who tried to do so generally failed.

The point being that intellectual property should always *serve* the business, not *be* the business. When I started the licensing program at IBM, Big Blue was on the ropes financially, with only a hundred days worth of cash on hand. Its most critical business need was revenue, and that's what we designed our IP strategy to generate. But when I went to work for Microsoft a decade later, Microsoft didn't need money—it had billions of dollars of cash in the bank. Instead, Microsoft needed to transform its relations with the rest of the industry and build collaborative relationships with other firms. So that became the focus of our new IP strategy.

Which sounded good in theory. But almost immediately after I accepted the IP job at Microsoft in June of 2003, that theory ran up against the harsh reality of the NAP (non-assertion of patents) clause—the same NAP clause that Gates and Myhrvold had designed to help save the company 10 years earlier. How we dealt with the new realities of NAP would be the true test of our new collaboration strategy.

Chapter 2

Like Cortez Burning His Ships

Microsoft has never been a stranger to controversy, as I was reminded less than a month after beginning to work, when I found myself in the midst of a major one.

I had gone to Tokyo to meet with several Japanese companies. One evening, during a dinner with senior executives from a large Japanese consumer electronics company, one of their vice chairmen suddenly leaned forward with a decidedly unfriendly look on his face.

"Your NAP clause is monopolistic," he announced loudly. "It is unfair, and we will fight you over it."

I didn't answer at first—not least because I had no idea what the NAP clause was. Apparently he took my stunned silence as resistance, which angered him even more.

"How can a man like you work for such a monstrous company?" he shouted.

I looked around the table at the firm's other executives, expecting to see in their faces the same shock that I felt at this man's confrontational behavior. Instead, their eyes were fixed on me, waiting for a response to a question they clearly thought deserved an answer.

"I'm sorry," I finally stammered. "I am not familiar with this NAP clause you mention. But I promise you I will look into it immediately upon my return to the States."

And with that, dinner resumed as if nothing had happened. But I knew that whatever this NAP clause was, if it could make senior Japanese business executives this angry—and they are normally courteous and nonconfrontational to a fault—I had better look into it soon.

As I discovered upon my return to Redmond, the NAP (non-assertion of patents) clause had long been a bone of contention in Microsoft's relations with the technology industry, both foreign and domestic. Devised by Bill Gates in 1993, when software patents were still rare and Microsoft lacked a patent defense against infringement claims by other companies (see Chapter 1), the NAP clause required PC and device makers, and other original equipment manufacturers (OEMs) who licensed Windows, to agree not to sue Microsoft or each other for patent infringement after they had already begun shipping a new version of Microsoft's software. If they felt that any of their patents were being infringed, they could not wait an extended period—or "lie in wait," as it were—for the new software to be shipped in large quantities around the world, and then demand correspondingly larger damage awards.

Apart from the fact that some OEMs found Microsoft's NAP clause unilateralist and galling—if they wanted Windows, they felt they had no choice but to accept the clause—they also objected to the immunity NAP granted to their own competitors in the global Windows ecosystem. If Sony believed its audiovisual patents, or if HP believed its printing patents, were being infringed by another OEM's deployment of Windows, neither could seek redress after shipment had begun, when damages would likely be greatly increased.

Interestingly, the European Commission and the U.S. Department of Justice had both reviewed the NAP clause in response to OEM complaints, and both had concluded that it was proper, given that it permitted OEMs to raise infringement complaints and even file lawsuits as long as they did so in a timely way. The Japanese OEMs, however, were not comfortable with this outcome, and so had brought their complaints to the Japanese Fair Trade Commission.

It's important to recognize, as I note in Chapter 1, that the NAP provision was entirely defensive in nature—a way not only to reduce the growing number of patent infringement claims targeted at Microsoft's increasingly deep pockets, but also to ensure some measure of patent peace within the PC industry as well. Indeed, in some ways it was not all that different from other "mutual defense" mechanisms in the industry, such as the Open Invention Network founded in 2005 to protect open source software companies from certain kinds of patent claims.

At the time that I started examining the NAP clause in late 2003, Microsoft had just been hit with a whopping 90 percent increase in the number of patent suits filed against it—from 19 in 2002 to 36 in 2003. This was the largest number of suits filed against any company in our industry, and as a result, we were now spending upwards of $100 million a year in legal costs to defend ourselves against such suits. The increase in patent suits was partly due to the bursting of the dot-com bubble two years earlier, which had led to the bankruptcy of many firms whose only remaining assets were their patent portfolios. Seizing on that fact, a number of law firms and other entities developed a new business model designed to monetize these patents by filing lawsuits. While this trend did not involve suits by PC makers themselves, it did point to a more litigious time ahead for patents relating to software.

Then, too, in August 2003, a jury in federal court in Chicago returned against Microsoft the largest verdict ever rendered in a software patent case—a $521 million damage award in the Eolas case. Concluding that we had solid grounds for appeal, we moved forward to appeal the case, and that appeal was eventually successful. But in the fall of 2003, our appeal was only a bet, and not yet a reality, and the original verdict clearly pointed to growing risks on the patent front.

Other suits were also pending, including one filed by Intertrust (a company backed by Sony and Philips) that could have resulted in a $1 billion-plus damage award. And those were the days when injunctions were often granted by the courts against the sale or distribution of products determined to have infringed patents. In many cases, therefore, Microsoft faced the threat of not only having to pay huge settlements or damage awards, but also of having the lifeblood of its entire business—the Windows and the Office suite of software—taken off the market.

Despite the defensive intent of the NAP clause, however, many in the industry viewed it as unfair. Not all felt that way: Newer OEMs as well as start-ups strongly supported the NAP clause. They did not have large numbers of relevant patents themselves, so for them NAP was a form of protection that had helped maintain "patent peace" in the PC industry throughout the decade of NAP's existence. OEMs with large patent portfolios, however, did not like the NAP clause because they believed it restricted their freedom to decide when and how to raise an infringement claim. These OEMs were actually fewer in number, but they were very important customers for Microsoft and they were very influential politically.

Another factor in the NAP policy was a move we had made earlier in 2003, at our customers' request, to indemnify them without limit against any patent infringement claims filed by a third party for their use of any Microsoft product—a move later followed by others in the industry. While this move was welcomed warmly by our customers, it also meant, in the context of the NAP clause, that if patent peace with the PC manufacturers fell apart and they started suing our customers, then Microsoft's liability risk would increase even more.

With this complicated situation as a backdrop, I asked my team in IP&L (intellectual property and licensing) to review the clause and get feedback from our most trusted OEM partners as well as internally. As I've noted, opinion in the OEM community was divided. There were also sharp differences of opinion internally, especially among the lawyers. No lawyer, after all, wants to be the one whose signature leads to a billion-dollar lawsuit against the company. So it was only natural that some of our attorneys expressed strong reservations about abandoning the (counterproductive, in my view) protections of NAP.

What to do? Although I had been making decisions since my first day at Microsoft, I realized that this one went to the very heart of Microsoft's efforts to build better relations with the industry. Incremental revisions of the NAP clause would not be enough, I felt. We had to make a bold, decisive break with the past and abandon NAP completely.

So in late 2003, after undertaking a review of all of the company's options regarding NAP, my team and I went to see General Counsel Brad Smith in Building 34 on the Redmond campus and made our recommendation. He was surprised, but not for the reason I first suspected.

"I actually expected Marshall and the team to come back and propose some relatively modest modifications," Smith told my co-author. "But Marshall and his people were telling me, 'You should get rid of this. Just get rid of it entirely!' And it occurred to me that this was one of the great things that Marshall had brought to the team—the ability to think without blinders, to look at issues in a fresh way without all the baggage of the past. But I was especially surprised that a team of lawyers that typically focuses on managing and reducing IP risks would recommend abandoning NAP, which among all the options considered, was clearly the most far-reaching and risky course of action."

At the conclusion of the meeting, Brad told us that before he could endorse such a bold move as abandoning NAP, he wanted to think it over and then run it by Bill."

Which he did. "Ultimately I concluded that the recommendation made a lot of sense," Brad recalls. "But it was not a lopsided decision. The NAP clause had proven its worth for a decade by preserving a strong measure of patent peace in the PC industry for software-related innovations. However, peace was coming at an increasing cost, in the rising dissatisfaction from the Japanese and some other large hardware manufacturers."

As for discussing NAP with Bill, Brad recalls what happened. "I was on vacation at Whistler [Blackcomb, in British Columbia], literally putting my ski boots on, when I got a call from Bill's assistant saying he was available to talk," Smith recalls. "So I walked out and stood in the snow for the next hour, talking to Bill. And at the end of that call, he agreed that we would drop the clause."

According to Brad, Bill's chief concern during the call was whether or not we had a new strategy to replace NAP in managing the risk that OEMs might sue us for patent infringement. So Brad outlined the cross-licensing strategy that I and my team were already developing, which was to use our rapidly growing patent portfolio to attract PC manufacturers, especially those with large patent portfolios, to enter into patent cross-licenses with us. During the conversation, Brad said, Bill tested the degree to which we had really thought this through and had a reasonable expectation of success. He concluded that we did, indeed, have a viable alternative to NAP—a fact later proved by our successful cross-license agreements with such major OEMS as Toshiba, NEC, Samsung, Siemens, and others.

In the end, killing the NAP clause proved to be even more significant internally than externally. "For us, it was the equivalent of Cortez burning his ships at the shores of the New World," Brad explains. "There would be no turning back now."

A Cultural Revolution

But others, it seemed, had second thoughts. For months after we scrapped the NAP clause—after Microsoft's employees had been notified by e-mail of the decision, after we had rewritten the Universal Terms Agreement with all our OEMs, and even after the company had publicly announced NAP's termination—zombie reincarnations of the dead NAP clause kept finding their way into the drafts of various agreements. Lawyers are trained to mitigate risk, after all, and not only were they reluctant to give up such a potent risk mitigator as NAP, but the simple act of changing long-established practices was itself considered risky.

And therein lies a critical point: change is a difficult, protracted, and intensely human endeavor. Companies don't change their business practices. People do. And it isn't accomplished simply by someone issuing an order or writing a memo or making an official pronouncement. Although it would have been hard to imagine a major change in Microsoft's strategy that did not have Bill Gates' support, not even he could make change happen simply by issuing an edict. Indeed, changing a company's business strategy is not unlike changing a country's political direction—it requires a convincing and compelling reason to do so, and the willing if not enthusiastic support of the majority of the company's (or the country's) citizens for making that change.

I was very conscious of this fact as I began the task of crafting a new intellectual property strategy for Microsoft. It has become fashionable in the IP world to talk about the need for companies to appoint a chief intellectual property officer (CIPO) with a clear executive mandate for maximizing the utilization of IP assets. And, to be sure, I did have a clear mandate from Microsoft's senior leadership to develop a world-class IP function that could facilitate new business opportunities and greater collaboration with the rest of the industry.

But I was also acutely aware that an executive mandate and a dollar will barely get you on the bus unless you also have the active support of middle managers, business unit leaders, and the key employees responsible for technology development, legal affairs, and relations with outside firms. It is they who have to be convinced that the vision you are charting is the right one, for they are the only ones who can implement that vision in the real world—where the rubber of corporate strategy meets the often-bumpy road of products, markets, customers, partners, and competitors.

The first challenge, of course, was to develop a patent portfolio that could attract other companies to want to establish cross-licenses and other collaborations with us. Despite running the largest R&D operation of any company in the world, Microsoft still ranked only 34th in the number of patents issued. This meant, first and foremost, that the company wasn't adequately protecting its most strategic technologies. But the modest size of our patent portfolio—perhaps 10,000 issued and pending patents worldwide when I arrived, compared to 55,000 today—also meant that we had insufficient options available for extracting value from those technologies, whether that be in the form of revenue from licensing, freedom of action for our businesses, defense against infringement suits, or collaborations with others that could enable us to acquire the new technologies and tap the new business opportunities we would need to succeed in the new "open innovation" environment.

Beyond the very practical challenge of increasing the size and strength of our patent portfolio, I realized at my very first meeting with the IP&L team in June of 2003 that we also faced some cultural challenges in developing a collaborative IP strategy. There were 16 people in the conference room, many of them sitting with their laptops open and frequently glancing at their screens to check e-mail. I felt as if I could have walked into that room naked and no one would have noticed. I later learned that this was common practice at Microsoft and indicated no disrespect. Still, the first thing I did was to ban laptops from my meetings.

But as I quickly discovered, this was merely one manifestation of a broader insularity and asocial outlook within Microsoft's corporate culture. Indeed, long-time company executives have told me that Microsoft had actually lost deals in the past because of the standoffish and introverted behavior of some of its employees. This would obviously have to change if the IP&L team was going to be able to win broad internal support for a broad-scale licensing program, let alone negotiate partnerships, collaboration deals, and patent cross-licenses with the executives of hundreds of domestic and foreign companies.

Microsoft's insularity manifested itself in other ways as well. Although the company had played an active role in many domestic and international IP forums over the years—including Susan Mann's excellent work in the company's Washington, D.C., policy office and Tom Rubin's work in the copyright realm—I felt there was an opportunity for Microsoft to broaden its thought-leadership role in such domestic and international IP policy debates as patent reform, the legitimacy of software IP, and the role that IP plays in innovation and economic development around the world. For a company like Microsoft—the largest software company on earth, with the largest R&D budget of any private enterprise in the world—a more active leadership role on IP matters was essential.

The need to overcome the insularity of Microsoft's culture also informed my work on organizational questions. Aside from rationalizing and streamlining the IP&L organization—reducing my direct reports by roughly half while at the same time bringing in certain functions such as our work with standards organizations, which naturally belonged in the IP&L portfolio—I saw the need to elevate more communicative, outward-looking people to positions of responsibility. I selected Bart Eppenauer as chief patent counsel to lead an intensified patenting effort, expanded Tom Rubin's copyright and trade-secret leadership to include trademarks, and asked Lisa Tanzi to oversee licensing. Among other members of the team to whom I gave new responsibility was David Kaefer, a gifted strategist and communicator notwithstanding his relative youth. I also brought in a few outsiders like Tanya Moore, who used to be on my team at IBM, and Mike Ward, who had been a senior executive at Honeywell and IBM. Both had the licensing expertise and the people skills that we critically needed. Within the first year we grew the staff by 50 percent.

We also tried to broaden the outlook and leadership horizons of the IP&L staff. I organized an internal "IP Summit" and brought in speakers such as former Commissioner of Patents Bruce Lehman and Ken Dam, who at the time was deputy secretary of the Treasury. I also urged members of the group to get much more involved in key IP professional organizations such as the Licensing Executives Society (LES), the Intellectual Property Owners Association (IPO), and the American Intellectual Property Law Association (AIPLA). I was convinced that if we couldn't hold our own intellectually in the policy and professional debates of the intellectual property community, we'd never get anywhere.

As Bart Eppenauer recalls, "You were constantly reminding us that we were all breathing from the same exhaust pipe, that we were too Redmond-focused and insular, and that we had to get out there in the wider world and learn how to engage with people as thought leaders."

The point being that business strategy always involves a cultural component. And the simple truth was that we would never be able to build a more collaborative intellectual property and business strategy unless we also created a more outward-facing and extroverted culture. This understanding was reflected in the "5 Year Plan" that we put together in those first few months, which called for us to achieve the following six objectives:

1. Build an outward-facing IP and licensing culture within the company.
2. Play a leading role in the global intellectual property debates.
3. Develop closer coordination between the IP group and the technical development teams in the business units to help guide innovation strategy.

4. Better protect our technologies by becoming one of the top-10 U.S. patentees.
5. Maximize our utilization of IP assets to support the company's business goals, standards efforts, and relations with open source and other firms.
6. Use licensing revenue and cost optimization to fund IP&L's expanded efforts.

Any sound business strategy, of course, must offer a strategic rationale that not only accurately reflects current economic, technological, and market conditions, but also clearly illuminates the benefits to be gained by its implementation. And here we put forward a vision of rapid and increasingly fragmented technological change in which collaboration with others, rather than the pursuit of market hegemony, would henceforth be the key to success.

Why Collaborate?

Today we call this theory "open innovation"—a term coined by Berkeley professor Henry Chesbrough in his 2003 book of the same name. Although we had not yet heard this term when we were developing our new IP strategy, we nevertheless embodied its essential elements in our "5 Year Plan," as the reader can see in Exhibit 2.1.

In our view, the creation and utilization of intellectual property was part of a virtuous circle in which R&D leads to the creation of IP, which leads to the licensing of that IP for valuable consideration—whether that be in the form of licensing revenue, rights to outside technology, or useful collaborations with other firms, such as the patent cross-licensing deals (PCLs) we signed with companies such as Nortel and SAP, which

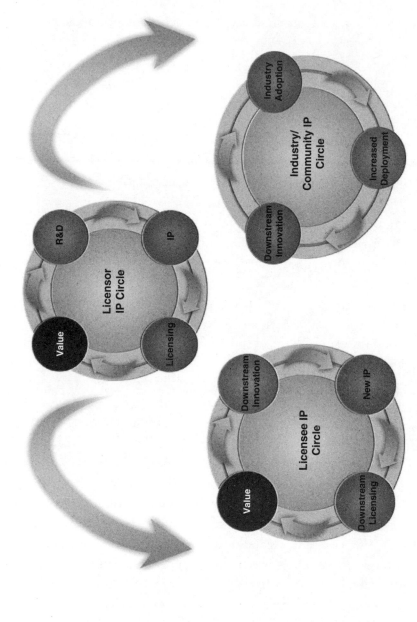

Exhibit 2.1 An Early Vision of "Open Innovation"

enabled us to conduct broader product-level collaborations. This in turn leads right back to new R&D, more IP creation, and so on. This virtuous circle then creates additional virtuous circles in the innovation behavior of firms that license our IP, for it enables them to enhance their own R&D, which leads to their own increased IP creation, which then provides them with their own downstream opportunities for licensing and value creation. Finally, these virtuous circles cascade throughout the industry, leading to the wider adoption of the licensed technologies and additional innovation. The key point here is that all these virtuous circles of innovation and value creation have as their central driving engine the collaborative use of intellectual property.

In short, we intended to turn the traditional paradigm for deriving value from intellectual property completely on its head. Instead of concentrating on tapping IP's *exclusivity value*—that is, using it to block competitors from using our technology—we would focus on leveraging intellectual property's *inclusivity value* in order to build the collaborative relationships we would need to remain successful in the new open innovation world.

And make no mistake: Collaboration is not merely a public relations function. It enables a company to more broadly and rapidly disseminate its technologies and products into the market through the cooperative efforts of others. It provides the framework for pursuing joint product development work with other companies that can lead to greater success in the marketplace. It can facilitate entry into new markets, broaden freedom of action within a market (especially through PCLs), and provide access to needed outside technologies. And, of course, a company can generate revenue directly through patent licensing. In short, IP-enabled collaboration can materially enhance the bottom line of a company and serve the interests of its shareholders.

As I noted earlier, the first item on the agenda was to build up Microsoft's patent portfolio. It was simply too modest both in size and in technological strength to offer us a broad-enough array of opportunities to collaborate with other forces in the industry. Bart Eppenauer quickly became the main champion of the effort. In the Microsoft patent group, he started hiring in-house lawyers to draft the patents instead of relying on outside firms, which not only enabled us to do it less expensively but also with greater quality and strategic relevance, because these in-house patent drafters worked directly with our existing patent counsels who were embedded in and worked closely with the development teams. He also created a "virtual law firm" so that outside attorneys and paralegals could more cost-effectively handle such tasks as prior art searching. All these efforts resulted in a huge increase in both our patent filings and in the number of patent issuances, thanks in part to the higher quality of the patent applications. As a result, the patent group finally brought Microsoft into the ranks of America's top-10 patentees, which is where the world's largest software company and largest research organization naturally ought to be. And they did it in only four years, one year ahead of our "5 Year Plan" goal!

It's worth noting here that patent quality has long been an issue that has challenged both the software industry and the patent office. But Eppenauer's quality improvement efforts eventually resulted in Microsoft earning top ranking by two different organizations that track patent quality. In November of 2007 and again in December of 2008, the Institute of Electrical and Electronic Engineers (IEEE) ranked Microsoft the leader among all technology companies, up from seventh place in 2006. And in their January 2008 quality scorecard, the Patent Board ranked our patent portfolio number one in both Technology Strength and Science Strength.

Another new initiative that Eppenauer helped launch was something we call "forward invention" sessions. Several times each year we brought together some of our best technologists and inventors for day-long discussions. These sessions would include people with a wide variety of backgrounds, both from Microsoft Research and the different product groups, in an effort to get Microsoft's lead thinkers to focus on innovations beyond the next product cycle.

The IP creation process in the context of forward invention sessions is very different from that of the traditional invention process, for which the basic question is, "Can I patent this innovation that I'm working on in such a way that it will still be valuable in five years?" In the context of the forward invention process, however, the key question is, "What are we *not yet* working on that could become important in five or 10 years? Should we do some inventing in this space and develop some intellectual property that could give us a seat at the table of an exciting new opportunity?"

The possibilities were intriguing. So Bart, senior attorney John Weresh, and I got Bill Gates interested in the idea (more on Bill's unusual leadership role in IP matters in Chapter 5), and today it's a thriving cross-disciplinary effort at the company—and one that puts the lie to the myth that Microsoft is a follower, not an innovator. Indeed, forward ideation is already opening up important new opportunities not only for breakthrough inventions but for collaboration with other firms as well.

As John Weresh noted, "I got a call from a representative of a huge company involved in an industry in which we've never had any business. It seems people at this company had read one of our published patents arising out of a forward ideation session and had some ideas about how we could combine our innovation efforts to make dramatic and possibly very lucrative breakthroughs. This is the sort of opportunity that we would never had a chance to pursue were it not for forward ideation."

It's also a perfect example of why, in the age of open innovation, it's so crucial to tap the *inclusivity value* of intellectual property and use it to foster collaborative relationships.

How to Build a Licensing Operation

With the portfolio-building operation launched, organizational questions settled, cultural reform underway, and our strategy clear in mind, it was time to develop the "Open for Business" licensing campaign that would serve as the engine of transformation for a new and more collaborative Microsoft. The key question here, of course, was whether or not the company, in the words of the industry magazine *Red Herring*, was truly ready to "abandon its fortress mentality around its intellectual property and open up channels of collaboration."

And this is where the real drama began.

In the first place, the very idea of "sharing" technology with others, especially one's competitors, ran counter to the basic modus operandi of a company that had for the last quarter century built its success upon the achievement of unrivalled market dominance and the jealous protection of its crown-jewel technologies. Indeed, Microsoft was perhaps the quintessential example of a go-it-alone company for whom competitive advantage had always been defined as "I've got it and you don't." The notion that competitive advantage could also mean, "I've got it and you've got it, and we're both better off for it" was simply not part of the company's DNA.

So, as you might expect, there was quite a bit of resistance to the notion of a broad licensing effort, especially from within the business units.

"You had people saying, 'Why should we share our technology with others, especially those who might be competing with us?' " recalls Bart Eppenauer. "They'd tell you, 'We worked hard on that, invested a lot of money and effort in it. So why give it up?' I mean, you could understand where they were coming from."

But there were other objections as well, says Eppenauer: "Even if you say that by licensing a technology you can build a relationship with another company and maybe even make a little money besides, the business unit leader might say, 'Not with my technology! We may not have any product plans for it now, but what if we need it later?' "

This "not with my technology" attitude was widespread, says Tanya Moore, General Manager for Outbound Licensing. "Historically, the business groups owned the technology they invented," she explains. "So their attitude was, 'Who are these outsiders telling us what to do with our own technology?' It took a lot of work to get people to look at IP as a *corporate* asset—and IP&L as the custodian of the company's patent portfolio—and to view a balanced licensing program as not only in the interests of their own group but of the whole company as well. And, by the way, that struggle is still going on—it'll always be there."

There also seemed to be little appreciation in some circles for the benefits that can be found in partnering with other firms. "There's often this attitude on the part of people here that they're so busy with their work, they don't have time for relationships," notes Weresh. "It was part of this whole asocial culture here. My response to this was to argue that if the company didn't start building industry relationships—and soon—there might not be any work for them to do."

Finally, Microsoft's own creation myth ironically led to one of the most potent sources of resistance to licensing. "No one wanted to be the guy who signed off on letting the next Bill Gates get a hold of the next DOS operating system," explains David Kaefer, who was director of business development for IP&L at the time and now directs IP licensing. "This is part of the founding story of Microsoft. It's bred in the bone of every Microsoft employee that, but for the deal that IBM signed with Gates in 1981 that allowed Microsoft to retain the IP rights to the DOS operating system, there might be no Microsoft today and IBM would own the market for personal computer operating system software. So yeah, no one wants to be the guy who gave away Manhattan for twenty-four dollars."

But for all the resistance to technology sharing, there were also powerful wellsprings of support for greater collaboration, some of which had been bubbling up within Microsoft since long before I arrived. Perhaps the most important of these was the ascendance of Brad Smith as general counsel of the company more than a year earlier. At that time, Brad had sought, and won, an express mandate from Chairman Bill Gates and CEO Steve Ballmer to reform three critical arenas of corporate policy.

"The first area," says Brad, "was antitrust policy. We wanted to do more to try to end our stormy relations with governments and with some in the industry. I had seen the toll that the antitrust suits had taken, not only on the company and its reputation, but on the people themselves. And so I believed strongly that it was time to settle the antitrust suits, both government and private."

(A wise move, in my opinion. As I had learned during my days at IBM, fighting the power of the U.S. government is a costly and usually a losing proposition.)

"The second area where we wanted change," Brad notes, "was in the role and operation of legal and corporate affairs [LCA] itself. We needed to get closer to the businesses and become a more valuable source of support for them. In essence, we needed to focus a little less on risk mitigation and more on business development opportunities.

"And third," he adds, "we wanted to change the fundamental way we approached intellectual property at the company. We needed to become more entrepreneurial with our IP, and identify how we wanted to use it as a business asset. This included using IP as a tool to develop new commercial partnerships with other companies that could benefit both them and our own bottom line."

These three objectives were clearly outlined in the famous November 2001 slide that *Business Week* claimed earned Brad his job as general counsel. Although the magazine wrote that this slide contained only five words—"It's Time to Make Peace"—in truth it was rather more detailed than that, although its message was essentially the same. One noteworthy aspect of Brad's slide was his insistence that "each [of the proposed changes] would involve an evolution of LCA's culture."

Another source of support within the company for collaboration developed out of the company's .NET (pronounced "dot-net") initiative, launched in 2000 to create an open platform that harnessed the global network architecture of the Web. Early development efforts were unsuccessful, owing to the perception that the technology was closed, and this fact was not lost on many employees.

Then, beginning in 2001, there were the early overtures of research chief Craig Mundie to the open source community, which received strong support from the many employees who recognized that peaceful co-existence with this significant industry force was essential.

Within the IP organization, too, there had been some bridge-building efforts undertaken with other forces in the technology industry. In 2001, for example, Tom Rubin met with Stanford Law School professor and political activist Larry Lessig and began a dialogue about supporting his Creative Commons initiative, an effort to develop more flexible copyright licensing terms to meet the needs of today's digital publishing environment. Despite the fact that Lessig had been a "special master" appointed by the court at Microsoft's U.S. antitrust trial—and company lawyers had sought his removal for "bias"—Rubin and Lessig developed a collaboration that resulted not only in Microsoft's financial support for Creative Commons, but also in the eventual technical development of an "add-in" for Microsoft's Office software that allowed users to automate the creation of documents using a Creative Commons license.

The key point here is that I did not come to Microsoft and single-handedly beat some collaborative sense into the company. Rather, I was brought in by Bill, Steve, and Brad precisely because *they* wanted to move in a new direction. My job was simply to help guide the effort and make some critical breakthroughs, especially in the collaborative use of patents and other IP.

Open for Business

In any event, all of these tributaries of support within the company for a more collaborative business posture merged in the summer and fall of 2003 in the planning of Microsoft's "Open for Business" licensing campaign. This effort proceeded on two fronts: developing an organizational capacity for it, and defining the policies that would underlie it.

On the organizational side, we had to build out our structure from scratch, because the company had basically no licensing function at all at the time. To be sure, Microsoft had done a few pure IP deals, but it had no systemic capability in this area.

"Licensing is basically a business development function," explains Tanya Moore. "And the problem was that we had zero network internally, no deal pipeline at all. Before you can even think about engaging with another company, you have to engage internally and find technologies to license. That means going to the middle managers, the corporate VPs, and the people responsible for that technology and getting their buy-in."

Which, Moore adds, was not an easy task. "I was working for Lisa Tanzi, and she was tremendously helpful in telling me who the key people were, the key stakeholders whose support I would need. And I made liberal use of her name to open doors—Lisa being one of the smartest people in the company and widely respected. I also made sure to use the LCA (legal and corporate affairs) moniker in my e-mail address, because otherwise my e-mail might have gotten tossed in the bit bucket. But when people see the 'LCA' in your address, they'll think, 'Uh-oh, she's with the lawyers . . . did I do something wrong?' And they'll be sure to respond to you."

When meeting with the business leaders, says Moore, "I'd try to establish a personal relationship. You know, what's important to this person? How can licensing a certain IP package help advance their business unit's strategy, as well as help the whole company? And eventually I'd develop a relationship where this person would want to partner with me in licensing. Because you need their support not just in getting the IP. . . . You need their technical people to come with you to meetings with the licensee, to explain the technology and answer questions. And if we do a deal, we might need their people on a joint development team with the other company."

As Moore worked on developing the initial deal pipeline, meanwhile, David Kaefer was leading the formal effort to define our strategic and tactical approach to the campaign.

"It was still very unclear if the 'Open for Business' campaign would get off the ground or not," Kaefer recalls. "You have to remember, we had just settled the antitrust suits and many in the company were reluctant to sign up for any sort of self-imposed policy on licensing that we could be held accountable to. So we'd have these meetings, and there would be like 15 or 20 lawyers in the room arguing over whether or not we should commit to reasonable and nondiscriminatory licensing terms for all comers—or even whether we should commit to any stated policy at all. There was also a lot of debate over the royalty rates. Should we base them on a simple across-the-board formula—say, one percent of associated revenue for one patent, two percent for two patents, and so on up to five percent for five or more patents? Or should we see what the market would bear in negotiations with each firm? Finally, there was debate over which technologies we would commit to licensing, and whether or not we would license these to all parties—including firms that we knew were trying to clone our products."

Here, of course, Microsoft's participatory democracy had a positive as well as negative effect. On the one hand, it made people feel invested in the project and brought forth many good ideas. But on the other, it tended to bog things down as consensus was sought on every issue.

"It would be an exaggeration to say that one negative vote could have killed the program," explains Kaefer. "But it did tend to slow down decision-making and action. To give you an idea, we wrote up the first draft of the one-page licensing policy in July, but it wasn't until November that we had all reached agreement on its basic outlines."

As typically happens in companies, of course, much of the internal debate over policy took place outside of formal meetings, in the halls and lunchrooms of Building 8 on Microsoft's Redmond campus. Almost every day, we would have discussions in those hallways—sometimes even heated arguments—about everything from our approach to open source to whether licensing should be organized on a hub-and-spokes service model or centered in the individual businesses. Looking back on it, I'm surprised no one asked us to get a room.

As Lisa Tanzi told my co-author, "That's one thing we all really appreciated about Marshall's management style—he was very much a believer in 'managing by walking around.' He'd just stroll down the halls, stopping by people's offices to chat or engaging them in the halls. Some managers think it's enough to have an open-door policy—you know, stop by any time if you have a problem. Marshall went way beyond that. He sought people out."

I was also very conscious of the fact that I was new at Microsoft and not well versed in the way things get done at the company. So I encouraged the IP&L staff to beat me over the head—with a frying pan, if necessary—if I was not listening to their concerns. To this day, one of my favorite treasures is a frying pan that everyone signed and gave to me.

Perception versus Reality

As we neared the launch date for the campaign, probably the biggest concern was how the "Open for Business" campaign would be received by the industry. Would it be seen as an attempt to "tax" the industry—as a confiscatory move to maximize Microsoft's revenues at other companies' expense?

To try to gauge the expected response, Kaefer met confidentially with a number of industry analysts and partners. Some of the feedback we received was positive, but much of it revealed a woeful lack of understanding about intellectual property's changing role in the new "open innovation" environment. Historically, intellectual property had always been treated as a weapon of competitive warfare. The idea that IP could serve as a bridge to collaboration with other firms was a radical new concept to many industry analysts—and an unproven one at that.

In any event, given Microsoft's reputation, it was easy to see why so many senior people were deeply concerned over how the new licensing initiative would be perceived.

"I was at a meeting with our general managers in Europe in late November of 2003," recalls Brad Smith. "And I told them, 'Look, in two weeks we're going to announce this.' They all thought the reaction was going to be enormously negative—that people would perceive our being 'Open for Business' as simply an attempt to force them to do something they did not want to do. I had to convince them that this move had merit, and even more importantly, that it was not going to cause the sky to fall. They made a number of good suggestions on how we could improve our announcement by involving partners in it. These made a lot of sense, and I promised them we would pursue them. Together, we got the announcement closer to the finish line."

We also had our teams working around the world in the final two weeks before the announcement to prebrief other companies and ask for their endorsements. Some of these 15 major endorsements didn't arrive until literally hours before the announcement. These played a key role in underscoring for the press and the public the non-acquisitive nature of the program.

On December 3, 2003, the "Open for Business" campaign was launched. "Microsoft Corp. today announced an expanded intellectual property policy to provide the IT industry with increased access to Microsoft's growing IP portfolio," read the announcement. Reaffirming the company's commitment to provide the academic community with patents under royalty-free terms for noncommercial use, the announcement committed us to offer our technology to all comers on commercially reasonable terms to both further Microsoft's own business and foster greater innovation within the industry as a whole.

The reaction was, in retrospect, entirely predictable. Although many companies expressed support for the move, most of the press and many analysts remained dubious about Microsoft's real intentions. In a few cases, the response was decidedly hostile.

At a venture capital conference in Silicon Valley a few months after the announcement, for example, many in the audience were openly suspicious of the program, calling it everything from a head fake to an outright disinformation campaign. Sam Jadallah, a former vice president at Microsoft who had made his fortune and then gone off to become a venture capitalist, stood up and accused me directly of being either a liar or a fool.

"It's just a pack of lies!" he shouted. "You'll never do this. Even if you wanted to, you'll never be allowed to do it by Gates and Ballmer."

Ironically, I had just received a personal e-mail from Bill Gates (with a copy to Steve Ballmer) stating "It's impressive to see how far we have come during the time you've been here. The review showed strong progress on all fronts. The challenge ahead requires this great work!"

But the reaction from Jadallah and others at the conference made me realize, in a way I never had before, that given the ill will many felt for Microsoft, words were not and never would be enough. Only through our actions could we prove our readiness to collaborate.

Collaboration's Bottom-Line Benefits

Which was fine by me, as we had a lot of work to do. Having opened the floodgates of collaboration, an enormous torrent of interest from other firms in Microsoft's advanced technologies and the fruits of our world-class research suddenly came pouring in. At the same time, a similar storm surge of interest within Microsoft for partnering with other companies cascaded across the various business groups, eventually leading to a number of collaborations with firms both large and small.

One of our early deals was with a small startup called Inrix. "Microsoft Research had this predictive technology that Inrix wanted to use in mobile devices to provide drivers with traffic-flow information," Tanya Moore explains. "It turned into a great lesson in balancing the interests of different groups within our company. The people in research really supported the deal, but the MapPoint team, which was developing their own applications using GPS data to provide geographic data to drivers, was worried that we were giving away a technology they might one day want to use—and worse, that it might one day be used by Microsoft competitors. But on balance, we all decided that the company was best served by licensing it out."

This sort of balancing act isn't always easy. "I've been yelled at many times over the past five years," Moore laughs. "I'd get these calls from product managers saying, 'You're killing my business!' And I'd have to go try to ease their concerns, show them that the sky isn't going to fall if we let their technology go to another firm—that, in fact, it would be good for the company.

"The point," she emphasizes, "is that your first sale is always internal. Without buy-in from the people most responsible for the IP, you're not going to get anything done."

For Inrix itself, the benefits of the deal were substantial. The technology they licensed enabled it to accelerate its product development and launch by two years. Nor does the company have to direct its own development of the software to benefit Microsoft in any way.

As for Microsoft, the benefits of the Inrix deal went far beyond simply the revenues that it will ultimately generate—small change for a company like ours that earns a billion dollars in free cash flow every month. As Moore describes it, "The major benefit in this case was that by helping another company build its solutions, we created a positive experience of partnering with Microsoft. And it helped teach us how to work with other companies."

She pauses a moment and laughs. "You know, I always have to smile when corporate PR announces a deal like this. I mean, it's like a wedding, right? Everyone's on their best behavior, they're dressed beautifully, it's all flowers and champagne. But the actual care and feeding of that partnership—the day-to-day work of collaboration—is much more like a marriage than a wedding. It takes work, and compromise. Learning how to manage these partnerships is exactly what we need to be successful going forward."

As *Corporate Counsel* magazine would later describe the Inrix deal, "Almost everything about this initiative challenges conventional wisdom about Microsoft. The deal isn't going to make a pile of money, and that's not the point. The enterprise famous for fighting across the globe to protect its software code is now licensing it out—and training people to modify it. It just may improve the company's image and relationships in the tech community."

Indeed, in the more than five years since we launched the "Open for Business" licensing effort, there's been a sea change in Microsoft's relations with other companies. The company has signed more than 500 patent and technology collaboration deals with companies large and small around the world, many with competitors such as Apple (including a recent collaboration on the iPhone), IBM, Novell, and Nokia. We have also entered into collaborations with close to a dozen open source software firms. In addition, we launched a new IP Ventures unit that has put cutting-edge Microsoft technologies in the hands of small start-tups in America, Europe, and Asia (more on this in Chapter 3). And we formed an Interoperability Executive Customer Council (IECC) and an Interoperability Vendor Alliance (IVA)—the latter made up of over 50 companies—to improve the way our technologies work with those of other firms.

Especially noteworthy have been our efforts to work with major competitors. While it's true that Microsoft has a long history of making technology available to its platform partners—mostly for free or at a nominal fee—our deal-making efforts with major competitors required a lot of adjustment and maturation in Microsoft's culture and business practices. Our 2005 deals with Nokia and Symbian (and later on, with Apple), in which we licensed our Exchange ActiveSync Protocol to major phone competitors of our own Windows Mobile platform, were prime examples of how we learned to work with competitors for mutual benefit.

On the copyright front as well, the collaboration efforts headed by Tom Rubin and his team led to what the *Wall Street Journal* called "an unusual cross-industry accord" in October of

2007, in which Microsoft and Disney recruited a dozen high-profile technology and media companies to support a set of rules—called the User Generated Content Principles—that they have agreed to abide by to resolve the contentious issues involving the posting of copyrighted content on social networking sites on the Web.

And finally, in recent years Microsoft also began to share much more of its crown-jewel technology with others, culminating in our February 2008 decision to publish more than 30,000 pages of technical specifications for our most popular software products for others to use, a move which one analyst likened to "McDonald's releasing the recipe for its secret sauce."

To be sure, we have generated some modest revenues from these new efforts. But to put these in perspective, we have paid out orders of magnitude more money to license other people's IP and technology—hundreds of millions of dollars each year—than we will ever bring in by licensing out our own. The royalties generated from patent licensing, of course, do benefit the bottom line and thus are important. But this is not the most important goal of the program. There are other benefits from licensing that make an even greater contribution to the bottom line, such as our February 2005 deal with Nokia that advanced Microsoft's e-mail server business, and helped move Nokia from RealNetwork's media technology to that offered by Microsoft.

In the words of Horacio Gutierrez, the man who succeeded me in 2006 in leading the day-to-day operations of the IP&L group, the "Open for Business" program helped us "learn, sometimes painfully, how to collaborate across company boundaries for the benefit of customers as well as our shareholders.

Sometimes this has meant putting aside perceived self-interest in order to settle disputes. Sometimes it has meant learning how to work with new types of entities, such as government agencies or even small entrepreneurs in China. And sometimes it has meant figuring out ways to bridge the gap between the business models, technology development approaches, and even basic philosophies that have long divided us from the open-source software world. But in every case, we developed these new ways to use IP to promote intercompany collaboration because *it was manifestly and inescapably necessary* for us to do so if our company and our industry were to move forward in any sensible way."

The Media Takes Notice

The changes wrought within Microsoft by our collaborative new IP policy have not gone unnoticed by the media and analysts. They have begun to chart our transformation—although sometimes the coverage has taken a tone of mild surprise, as if they can't quite fathom a Microsoft that now "plays well with others."

In an article entitled, "Redmond's Open-Door Policy," for example, *Fortune* magazine noted: "Since its founding a generation ago, Microsoft has been famous (and famously reviled) for guarding its secrets as vigilantly as the former KGB. But in a series of surprising and little-noticed moves, the company has made an about-face. Call it glasnost in Redmond."

The *New York Times,* for its part, agreed that Microsoft has finally begun to "foster more amicable relations between the big software company and start-up companies, which have often regarded Microsoft as a threat."

But perhaps the technology news network CNET said it best when, in May of 2008, it ran an article entitled "Who *Hasn't* Microsoft Signed a Patent Deal With?"

As analyst Chris Swenson of the NPD Group put it: "This is the new Microsoft. It really is changing."

Or, in the words of analyst Rob Enderle of the Enderle Group: "Microsoft is in the midst of the biggest change it has undergone since it became a multinational company."

To be sure, no one should imagine that Microsoft has morphed into some sort of high-tech Mother Teresa. The company is still in business to make a profit, and—trust me—it remains a tough and able competitor. As Laura DiDio, a researcher at the Yankee Group, put it: "They're not Doctors Without Borders. They're not pulling lepers out of the gutter."

True. But what Microsoft has done is forge important new partnerships with companies all over the world and gain access to valuable new technologies and market opportunities. As a result, it is much better positioned today to profit from what we call the new "collaboration imperative" of today's open innovation world.

For myself, I don't think I fully appreciated when I began this job just how powerful a tool intellectual property would prove to be in reshaping Microsoft and its culture. Although I had developed a strong appreciation of intellectual capital's importance, not only in corporate and national wealth creation but also to the daily lives of technology workers—whether they know anything about intellectual property per se or not—I had never really given much thought to IP as a *social organizing force* within firms before I came to Microsoft.

For Brad Smith, the magnitude of IP's transformational power also came as somewhat of a surprise. "Certainly, I knew that intellectual property would be of help to us in recasting our relations with the industry," he observes. "But I don't think I could have predicted the degree to which it has served that role so powerfully or effectively."

Having demonstrated that intellectual property could help fashion a new Microsoft, it was time to see if the risky bet we had made in abandoning the NAP clause would pay off in the form of successful collaborations with the world's largest companies—and with the world's smallest startups as well.

Chapter 3

Money Isn't Money Anymore

Two people. Two very different strategies. One goal—create new forms of value from intellectual property.

■ ■ ■

At precisely 10:00 A.M. on February 21, 2005, Anne Kelley and her four-person negotiating team sat down uneasily at one end of a conference table at Toshiba's corporate headquarters in Tokyo. Across from them, the six Toshiba negotiators sat in silence, the expressions on their faces making it clear that they did not wish to be in that room discussing a possible patent cross-license (PCL) with Microsoft, a company the Japanese press routinely called "evil."

"We were all very nervous," recalls Atsushi "Yoshi" Yoshida, a young patent agent on Kelley's negotiating team who would later go to law school and become a Microsoft licensing executive. "This was to be our *omiai*—in Japan, we call this a marriage meeting, like a blind date or something—but it was not a good atmosphere. We could see on their faces that they were not enthusiastic at all about discussing a PCL with us."

Not a very auspicious beginning, thought Kelley, whose mission was to negotiate the first in what we hoped would be a whole series of patent cross-licenses with major Japanese companies. Six months earlier, I had chosen Anne to head the patent cross-licensing efforts. But the Toshiba negotiations would prove to be by far her most critical challenge to date.

Why Toshiba was so important deserves some explanation. After we abolished the NAP (non-assertion of patents) clause a year earlier (see Chapter 2), the IP&L team had made some good progress in launching new licensing programs and entering into a number of new deals. In the second half of 2004, we concluded roughly 20 new deals, including patent cross-licenses with Cisco, Samsung, Autodesk, and Citrix. But the progress was very slow with the PC manufacturers in general, and with Japanese companies in particular. Because the linchpin for our strategy to replace the NAP clause was to sign patent agreements with PC manufacturers and OEMs, this was worrisome.

On February 3, 2005, my team and I held our annual midyear review meeting with General Counsel Brad Smith in Building 43 on the Redmond campus, and the discussion soon turned to the lack of progress in Japan. Anne Kelley, given her new responsibilities in charge of negotiating cross-licenses, was naturally at the center of this discussion.

"I conveyed my concern in the meeting about the lack of progress in Japan," Brad recalls, "and I started to push

Anne and the team pretty hard on how and when we might improve this."

We all decided that it made sense to focus on one Japanese company, put all of our energy into getting a first deal done, and then use that to persuade the other Japanese companies that we did indeed have a lot to offer in a patent cross-license and that they should follow suit.

Toshiba seemed the best candidate of all the major Japanese players, given that we already had a strong business relationship with them and held them in very high esteem, not to mention my own personal relationships with executives at the firm. In addition, we had also had some initial conversations on the patent topic in late 2004, which held out at least some promise.

Brad and I then pressed the team in the meeting to name a date by which they would seek to sign an agreement with Toshiba, offering to give them whatever executive support they needed. To everyone's surprise, Anne announced that she thought she could get a deal by March 31—less than seven weeks in the future! Seven weeks? Such deals, particularly with Japanese firms, typically take a year or longer to negotiate.

Brad recalls his reaction: "This seemed almost fanciful, since they had been trying to move things forward in Japan for almost a year without success," he explains. "But on the other hand, I had seen Anne sign up for seemingly impossible goals in the past and then surpass them."

Indeed, Anne had been extremely successful during the mid-1990s in the anti-counterfeiting area, after which Brad had asked her to start a new anti-piracy program aimed at increasing license compliance with larger customers. That, too, had been a success. In fact, shortly after I had arrived at Microsoft in June of 2003, Brad had recommended her to me as someone who could inject new thinking and enthusiasm into the IP&L team. After seeing her work, I had put her on point for handling the cross-licensing function.

So when Anne volunteered in the meeting that they would get a deal with Toshiba done by March 31, Brad and I jumped on the date and agreed that this should be the new goal.

As Brad put it, "It wasn't entirely clear that the rest of Anne's team was as optimistic as she was. But with her enthusiasm and Marshall's help, perhaps it could be achieved. At the very least we now had a specific plan that the team could pursue wholeheartedly."

Our objectives, once again, were first of all to demonstrate that voluntary mutual cross-licenses with Japanese firms could be effective in replacing the controversial NAP clause as a deterrent to patent infringement suits. We also needed to provide a kind of "existence theorem" for the value of our patent portfolio, and prove to large Japanese enterprises that we had a lot to offer in the way of technology collaboration. And finally, we wanted to redefine IP value itself, and demonstrate to both ourselves and the world that IP could generate far richer returns to the business than simply licensing royalties.

The problem was that our patent portfolio was still small compared to those held by companies of Toshiba's size and influence—a mere 5,000 issued U.S. and international patents compared to Toshiba's 18,000—and hence Toshiba might reasonably wonder what benefits a deal offered them. What's more, we were swimming against a strong current of anti-Microsoft sentiment within Japanese industry, a good deal of it generated by the NAP clause, which Japanese firms considered to be unfair and monopolistic.

Just one year earlier, in fact, agents from the Japanese Fair Trade Commission (JFTC) had staged what the press called a "predawn raid" on our Tokyo offices—it actually took place at 10:30 in the morning—looking for incriminating evidence of anticompetitive practices, especially with regard to the NAP clause. That we had already renounced the NAP clause even prior to the raid was insufficient, in the JFTC's view. It wanted NAP removed not just from future OEM agreements, but from all existing ones as well.

Early trial balloons to Toshiba around a cross-license had gotten us nowhere. But Toshiba finally agreed to have a team meet with us after I asked an old friend, a former Toshiba executive named Toshio Yajima who then worked as a Microsoft consultant, to arrange a meeting with Toshiba Senior Executive Vice President (and later CEO) Atsutoshi Nishida. As a result of that meeting, Nishida agreed to have his IP team sit down and at least hear what we had to say.

"We had a lot going against us in that meeting," recalls Kelley. "Apart from the NAP problems and our reputation as IP newcomers, we also had some major cultural differences to bridge. I mean, just having two women leading the negotiations—myself and Diana Dorr, who's now at Hewlett-Packard—was very unusual for these traditional Japanese executives. This just added to their discomfort and suspicion."

Which made it all the more important for Anne and her team, which also included senior Microsoft attorney Tim Carlson, to demonstrate that they were negotiating in good faith and willing to do whatever it took to create a fair and mutually beneficial collaboration with Toshiba.

"We did everything we knew how to do to show them that this was a new Microsoft they were dealing with," says Kelley. "We studied Japanese, we went to cultural training, and we constantly reminded ourselves that we needed to create a relationship, not just get a deal done."

Because this first meeting was taking place very soon after Valentine's Day, where the custom in Japan is for women to give gifts to men rather than the other way around, Anne and Diana presented the Toshiba team with award-winning Seattle-area wine and chocolates. (They would also later give one of the negotiators, whom they knew had young children, a gift of *anpan*—a sweet bun treat filled with a bean paste that is popular with Japanese children). Then they each made a few opening remarks in Japanese to their Toshiba hosts. This seemed to soften the attitudes of the Toshiba team—but only to a point.

"We were trying," Kelley remembers. "We were really trying."

Once the negotiations got underway, however, it was clear that Kelley and her team would have several hurdles to overcome. As expected, Toshiba asked why it was fair for them to share their very large portfolio of technologies equally with us, since ours was so much smaller. Kelley countered by pointing out that we had no need for patent coverage under certain of their technologies, such as their nuclear patents. In addition, she noted that while Toshiba's patents were more numerous, they were largely hardware based, whereas, going forward, the greatest mutual value would lay in software. Finally, team members stressed that although Microsoft's portfolio was still smaller than theirs, we had greatly intensified our innovation and patenting efforts and would soon have a very large IP portfolio to share with them.

"Your views are interesting," said Taisuke Kato, Toshiba's general manager of intellectual property and the leader of the Toshiba team. "We will consider them."

But when the talk turned to one specific issue—unfortunately, confidentiality agreements that Microsoft has signed with Toshiba specifically prevent me from identifying the nature of this issue—the negotiators hit a landmine. Suffice it to say that this generated the first real emotional heat in the discussions, with one of the Toshiba negotiators angrily announcing to Anne and her team "We can never accept your position!"

Thankfully, Kato then intervened and suggested that both sides consider the matter further and resume their discussions the next morning. If anyone on Kelley's team had hoped for an early breakthrough in the talks, they were sorely disappointed.

Back on the Home Front

Meanwhile, 5,000 miles away at Microsoft headquarters in Redmond, Washington, David Harnett was preparing to launch a collaboration initiative of his own—only this time with the world's smallest companies rather than the largest. A few months earlier, I had asked Harnett, a brilliant 33-year-old transactions expert in Microsoft's Corporate Strategy department, to develop a program to take early-stage technologies from our massive Microsoft Research (MSR) labs and "invest" these with entrepreneurs and small startups who could then develop these technologies into new products and services—and, ultimately, viable businesses.

The objective of this effort—which Harnett named "IP Ventures"—was threefold. First, the company wanted to generate more value from its enormous $7 billion a year research effort. Like most companies, Microsoft didn't employ all of the technologies it developed in actual products. The rest simply "sat on the shelf," as they say.

Harnett explains the rationale: "What do you do with all that research and applied research that falls through the cracks between our various product lines and businesses?

We had hundreds of people working on this stuff, and only a very limited outlet for it. That occasionally bothered the researchers, who like anyone else, want to see their hard work put to good use. And as a company, we wanted to get more value for all that innovation—whether that be revenues from a future application, relationships with entrepreneurs and venture capitalists, or whatever."

Then there was the value IP Ventures could generate through a process that IP&L Vice President and Deputy General Counsel Horacio Gutierrez calls "outsourced incubation."

"We have many technologies that are only at the concept or invention stage that need a lot more development to bring them to the point where they can become actual business applications with a real market," says Gutierrez. "If you're relying only on your own product road map, then a significant percentage of those innovations will never see the light of day. So what you want to do is to find a young company or an entrepreneur in a field where there might be a potential market for that technology—usually in a market we're not planning on investing in—and then you transfer the technology to them and help them develop and configure it into an actual product or service. The startup gets our technology and the expert assistance of our engineering teams, and we get the benefits of seeing how the technology tests out in the real world of products, markets, and customers. This is technically not 'incubation' in the traditional sense, since there is no intent by Microsoft to eventually acquire the licensee's business. But we do gain insights into other potential business applications of the technology by watching the licensee's real-life experiences in the field with it."

And finally, Harnett's goal was to use MSR's untapped intellectual property as a bridge to collaboration with the entrepreneur and venture capital (VC) communities, with whom

Microsoft had generally suffered from poor relations. Indeed, it was not uncommon at the time in Silicon Valley to hear Microsoft's attitude towards startups described by critics in three words: "buy or crush."

Harnett wanted to help build better relations with VCs and entrepreneurs not simply because he wanted Microsoft to be liked rather than disliked, but because better relations with the Valley could have great strategic value for the company. As noted earlier, the center of gravity of many kinds of innovation was shifting from large corporate R&D centers to dispersed networks of smaller firms and inventors. To get a seat at the table of some of tomorrow's more exciting opportunities, therefore, Microsoft needed to collaborate more effectively with entrepreneurs and with the venture capitalists who discovered and nurtured them. Simply put, Harnett wanted to narrow the distance between Redmond and Silicon Valley.

Good plan. But in meetings in Redmond and in Silicon Valley in late February of 2005 with Dan'l Lewin, who as Microsoft's corporate vice president of strategic and emerging business development knew the venture capital community inside and out, Harnett quickly realized he faced several roadblocks to getting IP Ventures off the ground.

In the first place, he had few if any entrepreneurs to work with, and as Lewin reminded him, "VCs don't invest in technology, only in the entrepreneurs who can build a business around it. To them, the team is far more interesting than the IP."

Harnett's second challenge, as Lewin was quick to point out, was that there would be no way the VC community would ever go for any deals unless they were structured according to "industry normal" terms. That meant, for example, that no one at Microsoft should expect VCs to pay cash for transferring the company's IP to a startup. Nor should they expect to have a right of first refusal should an acquisition offer later be made for that startup. In short, the "imperial dictates" approach that Microsoft had often employed in the past was out of the question here.

As Lewin remembers it, "I told David that it would be over my dead body that we would go to VCs with terms outside the industry norm, and he totally agreed."

And finally, Harnett knew better than most people how difficult it would be to get senior Microsoft executives to agree to share technology with firms that might one day compete with the company. He was, after all, the prime director of a corporate-wide assessment of intellectual property assets and utilization that I had commissioned from the Corporate Strategy department soon after coming to Microsoft. His study, completed in March of 2004, found that there was an enormous amount of technology and IP that was being created by the company but not getting utilized.

A key reason for this under-utilization, in my view, was a strategic mindset at the company that had long discounted the value of collaboration and technology sharing. My understanding is that the company had historically built its own strategy *against* that of its competitors. It did cooperate with other firms, to be sure, but in general the company focused most of its energies on competing, not cooperating.

So there wasn't a lot of interest in IP Ventures. Which was a problem, because to invest our technology with entrepreneurs, we were going to need the approval of the business groups that "owned" the technology.

How, then, to break through the barriers, both internally and externally? Harnett decided that even though he had no deals yet, he would announce the launch of IP Ventures at the upcoming annual meeting of the National Venture Capital Association (NVCA) in May, 2005. Maybe that would spark some interest and get the ball rolling. But he had no idea if it would really work.

The Unusual Friendly People

Back in Tokyo, meanwhile, Anne Kelley and her team were working at a furious pace. They met with their Toshiba counterparts almost every day, and then went back to their hotel and worked through much of the evening discussing the Japanese negotiating points and redrafting revised proposals to send over for the Toshiba team to consider the next morning.

"This was a much faster and more intensive pace than the Japanese were used to," Kelley notes. "Usually, it takes a year or longer to conclude a cross-license deal in Japan."

Ordinarily, this sort of push for a quick conclusion to the negotiations would have been resented by the Japanese. But there was something different about the attitude and behavior of Kelley and her team compared to past encounters the Japanese had had with Microsoft.

"We were always very respectful," says Kelley. "We listened to their concerns, tried to put ourselves in their position. We looked through our IP portfolio and tried to find technologies that would be useful to them, ways we could collaborate in media and other areas. We talked about how TVs were getting smarter, phones were getting smarter, and since getting smarter is really a function of software, we let them know about some of the more exciting software innovations we were working on that might be of benefit to them in the future."

Kelley's team also reaffirmed its support for Toshiba in its battle with Sony over DVD formats. As she put it, "We let them know that Microsoft would stick with them till the end." In the end, of course, Sony's Blu-Ray DVD format won out over

Toshiba's HD-DVD format. But Microsoft never reneged on its commitment to Toshiba.

"But the most important thing," says Kelley, "was that we really tried to break with the way Microsoft had often handled relationships before. You know, relationships with Microsoft had often been short term and very transactional—you do this for me, I do this for you. Over and out. But we wanted to build a relationship that was not limited to a particular deal or quid pro quo. We wanted a broader kind of collaboration, a true partnership, where we could work together in various areas and share our views about where the industry was going. We wanted to build bonds of trust that would, as they say, stand the test of time. And this was new for us—it was really a reflection of the whole cultural change going on at Microsoft at the time."

Indeed it was. Consider how different Kelley and her team's approach was from the way the NAP clause was imposed on Japanese companies. From the Japanese point of view, Microsoft had a de facto monopoly in Windows, with 95 percent of the market in personal computer operating systems. So if you wanted Windows, you had no choice. You simply had to accept the unilateralist NAP clause. And the Japanese deeply resented that.

Our new attitude helped pushed the negotiations forward, and at one point Kelley made a joke about how her team hoped to have Toshiba's signature on a deal by White Day on March 14, when Japanese men give gifts in return for the chocolates (*giri-choco*) that women had given them on Valentine's Day. But that was not to be. Instead of giving the IP equivalent of an engagement ring, the gentlemen from Toshiba instead took them out to a traditional Japanese restaurant. It was a nice, friendly, but noncommittal evening—much like that which a man unready to pop the question might enjoy with his date back in the States.

On and on the negotiating continued, through seven more grueling sessions. The question of payments was resolved, as was the capture date for future patent issuances that the parties would be entitled to under the cross-license. Only one issue remained—the roadblock issue mentioned earlier—and that was finally resolved late in the evening of March 31 in the time-honored manner in which diplomats down through the ages have always handled irresolvable issues.

Which is to say it was finessed. Because neither side could figure out precisely how to resolve the problem holistically, we agreed to put the issue at the margins in the interest of unity.

And with that Anne Kelley achieved a critical breakthrough in Microsoft's relations with Japanese industry. She had proved that Microsoft could collaborate with Japanese firms on fair and equal terms. And she had demonstrated that, even if our technology portfolio was not as large as those of some Japanese firms, we had a great deal to offer any potential partner in terms of advanced software technology and our future innovation capacity.

Recalls Brad Smith: "As you can imagine, we were all very pleased. When we spoke on the phone on March 31, the day the deal was signed, we all laughed about the fact the fact that Anne had signed up for what seemed like an impossible goal—and then had actually done it!"

Looking back on it, Kelley says, "We had two secret weapons in those talks. The first was this new mindset we had at Microsoft that favored greater collaboration. And the second was Yoshi [Atsushi Yoshida]. I mean, it wasn't just that he helped us navigate the language and culture and all that. He was the most brilliant, strategic, personable, sensitive, and intuitive guy. He could read the room, and because of that, he helped us make the right decisions."

Meanwhile, the deal secured the signatures of the various Toshiba division heads—a process known in Japan as *ringi*—and the Japanese government was informed of the results. When that process was completed, Anne Kelley and her team flew back to Tokyo and took their Toshiba counterparts out to dinner at one of the city's finest Italian restaurants for some much-earned celebration and a little *honne*—"belly talk" or "straight talk."

"Usually, Japanese people are *tatemae*," explains Yoshi. "They are reserved in their talk, especially with outsiders. But *honne* is for special occasions, when you express your true thoughts and feelings. So that night we drank cheers—*kampai!*—and we had *honne*."

Says Kelley: "Mr. Kato, the leader of their team, told us that at first he didn't think a broad cross-license made sense for our two companies. But he had been told by his senior executives that he had to meet with us. He said he felt differently, though, when he saw how we really tried to cooperate, even in challenging situations. The phrase he used was *doryoku*—'making the effort.' He said he appreciated how Microsoft had 'made the effort.'"

The "dessert," if you can call it that, came in the form of a Tokyo television news story about the Toshiba-Microsoft PCL. It might seem odd for a TV network to air a story on something as arcane as a patent cross-license, but the angle here was really Microsoft—always a newsworthy subject in Japan. The reporter went through the usual rehash of "evil" Microsoft behavior over the years, and then noted that the deal with Toshiba was due to a new attitude on Microsoft's part. He referred to Kelley's team as "the unusual friendly people at Microsoft."

Calling All Entrepreneurs

There is a good reason why David Harnett asked Dan'l Lewin to make the announcement of the launch of Microsoft's IP Ventures program at the May 4, 2005 annual meeting of the National Venture Capital Association. Lewin was a highly respected figure in Silicon Valley and the venture capital community, having lived and breathed its unique culture for more than 25 years. His career spanned stints first with Steve Jobs at Apple and then at NEXT, then as VP of marketing and sales at the mobile computer startup Go, and after that as CEO of the startup intellectual property asset management firm Aurigin Systems. If there's an important entrepreneur or venture capitalist who Lewin doesn't know, then he or she probably doesn't exist. Indeed, his entire career, and much of his social network and intellectual life, is infused with this intimate connection to high-tech startups and the venture capital community.

Lewin came to Microsoft via a rather serendipitous route. In late 2000, he read a speech that newly appointed Microsoft CEO Steve Ballmer had given about the importance his firm attached to XML (Extensible Markup Language), which was a technology that allowed disparate information systems to share structured data—words, pictures, anything—over the Internet.

Lewin, too, had been thinking about XML and its implications for the future direction of the technology industry for some time. "To me it suggested an evolution beyond the old binary client-server structure of computing," Lewin explains. "Its architecture was distributed. The data would be in the hands of anyone who owned it—didn't matter if it was a PC or a cellphone or a large corporate database—and it could be shared and moved around in any way you wanted. This technology would decentralize the market and allow people to share information in peer-to-peer social networks or across enterprises or whatever. Corporations could move information across proprietary databases—in effect, it would eliminate in some sense proprietary control.

"Bottom line," Lewin continues, "XML would greatly advance the possibilities for interoperability. Anybody could get in the game of developing applications that work with everything else—small startups, the lone programmer, or the biggest companies in the world. In a sense, I saw XML as a key technical embodiment of open innovation. And if Microsoft was committing to XML at the tools level, which is fundamental, then it had a huge opportunity to start collaborating in much deeper ways with startups and with the venture capital community."

So Lewin sent Ballmer an email asking if he was really serious about XML and all that it implied. Ballmer responded by inviting him up to Redmond, and on January 5, 2001, the two men sat down together in Redmond for a ninety-minute talk during which Lewin laid out his vision for how Microsoft should collaborate with VCs and the Silicon Valley community.

Four days later, Ballmer called Lewin at home and turned the tables on him. "What I want to know is," Ballmer asked, "are *you* serious? Because I want to make you an officer of the company. I want you to run our operations in the Valley and be our emissary there."

Today Lewin is the site executive for Microsoft's 2,000-man operations and research center in Silicon Valley, where he guides the company's approach to startups, venture capitalists, and emerging business opportunities not only in the Valley but all over the world.

In short, Dan'l Lewin is Microsoft's public face to the VC and entrepreneurial community—and, perhaps more important, that community's voice and honest broker within Microsoft. Harnett could hardly have asked for a better advisor and spokesman for IP Ventures.

So when Lewin made the announcement of IP Ventures' launch on May 4, 2005—and told the world that Microsoft was finally serious about reaching out to entrepreneurs and VCs and helping to launch some exciting new ventures—the news had an immediate impact.

"We got a much better reaction than I expected," says Harnett. "The press was actually overwhelming—and overwhelmingly positive, including a very positive piece in the *New York Times*. I got a lot of calls after that."

Ironically, says Harnett, the announcement also stimulated interest *within* Microsoft. "A lot of people internally contacted me right after we did the announcement," he recalls, "either with an idea for a technology that might make a good venture or because they wanted a job. These were people from all over the company."

Harnett laughs: "But it was funny . . . some people contacted me very quietly. They were afraid of appearing disloyal. They were afraid their managers would think that maybe they wanted to leave the company just because they wanted to work with entrepreneurs. Or that they were trying to help outsiders compete with Microsoft."

It was precisely these outsiders, these entrepreneurs, that IP Ventures needed to find—and soon—or the project would die on the vine. But where to find those who could be matched with the more than 20 Microsoft technologies that Harnett was assembling for transfer?

Less than two weeks after the announcement, Harnett was participating in a panel discussion on corporate spin-outs at the Corporate Venturing Conference in London. Afterward, he was approached by Gerard O'Flynn of Enterprise Ireland, a government economic development agency that fostered the development of Irish small businesses. He had heard that Harnett was Irish, had read about IP Ventures in the press, and was interested in working with Microsoft to foster partnerships with Irish companies.

Harnett quickly arranged to meet with O'Flynn and his divisional director, Michael Moriarty: "I told them, 'There's no point in talking about IP and business plans unless we can find really good entrepreneurs. Can you help us do that?' And they both said, 'Absolutely!' "

And with that chance encounter, one of the most unusual and productive government-industry collaborations in the history of entrepreneurialism was launched. Enterprise Ireland assigned its portfolio managers, who covered various technical disciplines, to study each and every one of the technologies in Harnett's stable. Then the Enterprise Ireland staff sent out flyers—as well as e-mails and phone calls—to hundreds of Irish startups and entrepreneurs working in related technology fields. Those who were interested were then prescreened to make sure that they had the bandwidth and business acumen for this sort of collaboration, eventually narrowing down the likely candidates for each of IP Ventures' technologies to a dozen or fewer.

"It was just terrific," says Harnett. "We could travel to Ireland and in just one day we could meet with all these very accomplished, already-vetted entrepreneurs. I mean, over the course of a couple of years, Enterprise Ireland reached out to literally thousands of entrepreneurs and startups on our behalf. They knew how difficult it was to take IP from the research lab and find the right entrepreneur who would be able to build a viable business with it. They were just amazingly efficient and effective. They knew how to build Irish businesses."

The first product of Harnett's partnership with Enterprise Ireland was a new Irish firm called Softedge Systems. Employing a Microsoft technology called Interactive Image Cutout, SoftEdge Systems today provides software products that allow nontechnical users to create multimedia documents and content.

A second Irish company that benefited from Enterprise Ireland's cooperation with IP Ventures was Vimio, which creates products that deliver video in low-bandwidth environments with clearer shape, smoother motion, and shorter latency on mobile devices.

Harnett soon expanded IP ventures' reach to include Europe, Asia, and the United States. In most of these deals, IP Ventures helped the entrepreneur to launch the company itself — incorporating the company, helping to secure venture capital financing, hiring the employees, writing the employment agreements, and doing everything else needed to set up a new business. All deals were organized along industry-normal terms, including taking an equity stake in the venture but receiving no cash for the transfer of Microsoft technology nor any right of first refusal in the event of a later acquisition offer. And unlike most venture capital deals, IP Ventures did not take a voting seat on the startups' boards, to ensure they could operate independently and make their own decisions free of our control. In many cases, IP Ventures licensed technology to startups that were already in existence.

European firms receiving Microsoft technology through IP Ventures included the UK firm Skinkers, which develops direct-to-desktop event notification and content delivery solutions, and Blucasa, a start-up in Italy, which licensed Microsoft's Mobile Video Optimization technology to improve the way mobile devices handle video communications.

In China, IP Ventures partnered with two Chinese companies—ComTech of Shenzhen, and TalkWeb of Hunan. ComTech licensed two technologies—called Mobile Picture and Mobile Bandwidth Optimization—for transferring and viewing videos on mobile devices. And TalkWeb licensed a technology called Personalized Facial Sketch that allows photos to be turned into cartoon sketches and then transmitted and displayed on mobile devices.

And in the United States, IP Ventures helped launch a Seattle, Washington, startup called Zumobi, which employed Microsoft technology to create a high-frame rate Zooming User Interface that allows users of mobile phones such as the Blackberry and iPhone to surf and share digital content quickly, easily, and in more compelling ways. IP Ventures also licensed Microsoft's patented "TouchLight" technology to a Mountain View, California, company called Eon Reality, which develops offerings that allow users to physically interact with 3-D visual content. And it invested an MSR social networking technology to help create a new Silicon Valley startup called Wallop, which aims to develop next-generation social computing applications.

In all of these deals, Harnett faced the challenge of overcoming years of "fortress mentality" thinking within the company. Indeed, even though the IP Ventures program had the approval and support not only of myself, but Bill Gates, Steve Ballmer, and Brad Smith as well, the battle to give it life still had to be waged in the trenches—in the business units that are the heart and soul of Microsoft and every large corporate enterprise.

"We had this policy where we had to get the approval of a corporate vice president from the business group that nominally 'owned' the technology," Harnett explains. "And we used to run into problems because this person usually had no incentive to say yes. In fact, his only incentive was really to say no, because after all you can never really guarantee 100 percent that one day in the future we wouldn't wish we had used the technology in our own products."

Harnett always got the approvals because, as he put it, "We really worked hard at it—playing up the business benefits of working with entrepreneurs and open-source companies and playing up the positive PR angle. And even though there was reluctance at times because it went against Microsoft's previous practice, in the end the VPs all agreed. If nothing else, they didn't want to be seen as interfering with the company's new commitment to collaboration."

"An Incredibly Rich Collaboration"

IP Ventures didn't simply make deals, or even help launch companies. It engaged in extensive high-value technical collaborations with the companies it worked with, as exemplified in the case of Zignals, a financial services startup launched in concert with Enterprise Ireland and the Irish entrepreneurs Pat Brazel and Scott Tattersall. Zignals' aim was to develop an online investing service that provided retail investors with state-of-the-art decision-support tools previously only available to major financial institutions.

"We had this incredibly sophisticated research technology that our mathematicians and engineers were working on called the Microsoft Solver Foundation, which can take in hundreds of thousands or even millions of variables and come up with optimal solutions," says Harnett. "For their part, Brazel and Tattersall were working on a financial services idea at Dublin City University's business incubator. After we started talking, we realized that our Solver Engine could be a powerful platform for their application. So it was like, 'We'll provide the motor, and you provide the chassis, wheels, and steering of a vehicle for a new kind of financial service.' "

The partnership they developed was unprecedented—at least for a company like Microsoft that had always been famous for the secrecy with which it guarded its technology assets.

"It was an incredibly rich collaboration," Harnett recalls. "I mean, during the development phase, each side was writing research papers and passing them on to the other side. And, you know, we're asking them, 'Guys, if we change this in the engine, will this help your application?' And if they said yes, then we'd modify the platform architecture—sometimes overnight—to meet their needs. Meanwhile, they're providing us with all sorts of valuable data on how this is all testing out with their beta customers in the real world."

According to Harnett, Microsoft engineers were especially thrilled with the project. "This is a very high volume, real-time application—exactly what the mathematicians and people building this type of engine really want to engage with. And don't forget, nothing makes a developer more happy than seeing an invention turn into a real-world product or service that changes people's lives. This is heaven to them."

So what was the benefit to Microsoft of this effort—other than making its researchers happy, of course?

"Well, from a financial standpoint, if we take a seven-to-ten year view of this—which is what you do in the venture business—then we may realize some value for our equity stake," Harnett explains. "We also gained valuable 'external incubation' experience for a platform that might one day have applications in a variety of consumer products and services. But to my mind, one of the biggest benefits is that we got a lot of entrepreneurs and companies looking at the fact that Microsoft can be a good partner, a good collaborator. That's key."

Indeed, it is of enormous long-term strategic value that tomorrow's young inventors look to Microsoft as a potential partner in creating the future innovations that may launch whole new industries and—who knows?—even change the world.

Microsoft also benefited by learning how to work with government economic development agencies such as Enterprise Ireland and the Finnish National Fund for Research and Development, known as Sitra, which help to grow local businesses and strengthen the whole ecosystem for information technology products and services.

As Frank Ryan, CEO of Enterprise Ireland, has noted: "IP Ventures furthers our ability to assist local businesses in an international market."

Indeed, in acknowledgement of IP Ventures' work in assisting Irish businesses, on July 16, 2008, Irish Prime Minister Brian Cowen presented David Harnett with the Meithel Award for outstanding contributions towards helping Irish companies succeed in the global market. Meithel is the Irish word for a "work group"—a band of people engaged in a common effort.

Value Greater Than Money

Life is funny sometimes. When I came to Microsoft in June of 2003 to craft a new open innovation–age intellectual property strategy, even I did not anticipate the degree to which the company would be transformed by it. And, even more ironic, I also failed to fully appreciate the extent to which open innovation itself would liberate intellectual property value creation from the tyranny of dollars-and-cents accounting.

After all, I had a reputation in industry and in the IP professional community as the man who had created a $2 billion a year pure-profit business for IBM through licensing IP that was just sitting in the company's legal filing cabinets. That's about as dollars and cents as you can get—and, indeed, no company on earth has ever been able to duplicate anywhere near that scale of revenue mining from its IP "Rembrandts in the attic."

And yet, when I look at what we have been able to accomplish in six years at Microsoft, I am struck by the extraordinarily rich and diverse forms of tangible *non-cash* value that we've been able to generate from this supposedly "intangible" asset class.

Consider, for example, our many dozens of patent cross-licenses with other companies. Following Anne Kelley's breakthrough with Toshiba, Microsoft signed more than 15 patent cross-licenses with major Japanese companies—one of the most interesting being the August 2008 PCL with Nikon that will enable the collaborative development of new digital camera products by both companies. Indeed, cross-licenses with major firms in Japan, Korea, and many other countries are proving enormously valuable not only in expanding our business through the creation of new consumer products, but also in providing greater freedom of market action for the parties to such deals.

Patent cross-licenses have also proved useful in opening up new market opportunities, as our collaboration with communications leader Nortel demonstrated. Three years ago, we were looking for a way to enter the unified communications sector, but lacked telecom experience. Nortel, for its part, was looking to do the same, but lacked next-generation software expertise. So in July of 2006, we forged a patent cross-license with Nortel to jointly develop new enterprise, mobile, and wire-line carrier solutions that close the gap between the devices people use to communicate and the applications they use to run their businesses. This PCL also involved major investments by both companies in collaborative marketing, business development, and sales.

In all those deals and many hundreds more, Microsoft sometimes received money, and sometimes did not. And sometimes we even paid money to gain access to technologies we needed—more money, in fact, than we're ever likely to make licensing out our IP. If our strategy had been governed by a strict short-term accounting ledger, we never would have gained the new business and market opportunities that we've been able to realize through these deals.

Our effort to create new forms of IP value also enabled us to sometimes turn risk into reward. "Most traditional corporate patent groups have a very limited set of tools they use when trying to manage potential or actual IP assertions by third parties," says Kenneth Lustig, managing director of IP acquisitions and investments within IP&L. "It's very binary, and the overriding motive is risk management. But when we looked at the increase in patent assertions and litigation from companies that were entirely different from those with whom we usually conducted patent cross-licensing agreements, we decided to broaden our approach at Microsoft. We wanted to move beyond risk management and instead treat these matters as opportunities."

Lustig played an interesting role in the development of our overall IP strategy. With a background in investment banking and experience leading acquisitions and investments for the company's corporate development group, he came to me soon after I arrived at Microsoft with a plan to apply some new capital market and other strategic tools to achieve our IP goals. He recommended the creation of an IP Acquisitions and Investments team under IP&L, and Bill Gates, Brad Smith, and I really liked the idea and signed off on it.

"The basic idea was to be creative rather than just follow the traditional approach of straight-in licensing or litigating," Lustig explains. "If we needed to get certain IP rights, or if we needed to play in a space where IP rights were critical, then let's see if IP investment strategies can help us—and maybe also help us make a little money besides."

The 2002 Immersion patent infringement suit against Microsoft is a case in point. Immersion specialized in something called haptic technology, which employs the sense of touch to expand the interaction between humans and computers. Its technology, originally developed at Stanford University, is used in joysticks that respond physically to elements in a video game—as when a joystick shudders after a player's jet fighter is shot in a flight simulation game, or vibrates heavily when a player puts the pedal to the metal in a car-racing game. The company claimed Microsoft infringed its technology. We had previously taken a limited-use license to use Immersion's IP in our force-feedback PC Sidewinder joystick. After we launched the Xbox gaming system, however, Immersion demanded a significant new royalty from us. Attempts at a compromise were unsuccessful, so Immersion sued.

Rather than simply battle the company in court—or just license the technology to settle the matter—in July of 2003 Lustig's group instead negotiated a multilevel agreement. As Lustig explained, "We liked the technology, and given we had already taken a partial-use license, we didn't want this case to go to trial. We thought that Immersion had a viable business and felt if we helped the company, we could end the dispute on a positive note."

In a deal involving a series of strategic and financial ar-rangements, we paid Immersion $26 million—which helped Immersion's stock price go up fourfold. The arrangement also entitled Microsoft to certain sublicensing payments in the event that Immersion settled a similar patent infringement suit it had filed against Sony, which it eventually did.

"It was a smart investment that also helped this promising company survive and thrive," notes Lustig, "and we also eventually received back $20.75 million in payments from the company, in addition to significant investment gains."

For the most part, though, IP acquisitions, investments, and in-bound licensing are designed not to produce a profit—at least not directly, or in the short-term—but rather to acquire needed technologies, build partnerships, achieve strategic objectives, and/or resolve disputes.

Consider, finally, the new kinds of business value gained through David Harnett's work with IP Ventures and Dan'l Lewin's ambassadorial role in the Silicon Valley startup and venture capital community. Their work with brilliant young entrepreneurs and venture capitalists all over the world has not only expanded our technological reach and given us entre into some exciting new business and market opportunities. It also made us much less likely to ever be caught flat-footed again when the Next Big Thing emerges on the high-tech landscape. More than anything else, perhaps, Harnett and Lewin truly have greatly improved our relationships in the Silicon Valley community.

"I remember when I first joined up with Microsoft in 2001," recalls Lewin, "many of my friends said, 'Hey, you joined the dark side!' I mean, that was the sort of antipathy that existed towards Microsoft at the time. And you could see it in the polling results I got after the first Microsoft VC Summit I organized that year."

Of the 80 VCs who attended that summit and anonymously filled out Lewin's survey in 2001, 62 percent said that Microsoft would *not* be a good partner for their portfolio companies.

Only 39 percent wanted their companies to collaborate with Microsoft.

By 2008, however, the community's perception of Microsoft had changed dramatically. Of the 165 VC Summit attendees who responded to Lewin's survey that year, 80 percent, or 131 people, said they would definitely or probably recommend Microsoft as a business partner to their portfolio companies. Twenty-six people said they might recommend the company, and only four people, or 2 percent, did not want Microsoft as a partner (with another 2 percent saying they had no opinion).

What a difference a new IP strategy makes—especially when it's part of a broader transformation in business strategy and practices.

"One thing you can say about Microsoft, we never play for second place," laughs Lewin. "When we were first trying to build a business in the emerging new software market, we were the best. Now, when collaboration is the name of the game, we want to be the best at that, too."

He pauses a moment, reframing Microsoft's behavior from a developmental perspective.

"Look, there's nobody on the planet who builds software on the scale that Microsoft does or competes in global markets as strongly as we do," insists Lewin. "There are some very, *very* smart people leading our business units and product groups. But at some point you've got to put aside that Excel spreadsheet you have in your head, and step outside yourself and see how other people see you. That's the wisdom component that every person or business needs to have. You've got to be able to say, 'Okay, we can't go it alone anymore. We need to mature. We need to create a business environment where people will want to partner with us.' Because that's how you do business effectively today."

Having successfully used intellectual property to create valuable new business opportunities with both the largest and smallest companies in the world, the next challenge was to use IP to break through the logjam of animosity and mutual suspicion that had long divided the proprietary and open source software worlds. But could we truly bridge the gap between our very different business models and software development approaches?

Chapter 4

A Very Secret Mission

S usan Hauser did not at first glance seem like an ideal candidate for a confidential mission to help Microsoft secure an intellectual property peace agreement with the open source software community.

For one thing, she didn't know a thing about intellectual property. Nor was she a lawyer, trained in the arts of confidential negotiation. Rather, the gregarious 46-year-old wife and mother of two high school–age sons had spent all of her 15 years at Microsoft working in sales, building and managing relationships with large customers. A psychology major in college, she had gotten her teaching credential and spent five years after graduation as a special education teacher in the South Bronx before pursuing her second love—technology—and hiring on at Microsoft, where she rose to the position of general manager of sales for New York and New Jersey.

But there was a reason that CEO Steve Ballmer, on one of his periodic visits to meet with East Coast customers, had called her into a private conference room at Microsoft's offices at 1290 Avenue of the Americas one day in April of 2004 and closed the door.

"Customers respect you," he told her. "And even more important, they trust you. And for this assignment, we're definitely going to need someone our customers trust."

Ballmer then revealed the broad outlines of "Project Summer," a high-level confidential initiative within Microsoft to forge the first intellectual property and technical collaboration agreement between a major proprietary software company and a major distributor of open source software. In short, Microsoft wanted to cut a deal with an open source vendor such as Red Hat, the market leader in Linux software for large enterprises, or Novell, the number-two player, that would improve the interoperability of the Windows and Linux software systems and also relieve customers of any concerns over intellectual property licensing requirements.

The reasons why this initiative was called "Project Summer" are somewhat murky. Some sources within Microsoft insist the name derived from the company's original plan to license its IP directly to a number of customers by the summer of 2004—while at the same time pursuing the longer-term hope of a bilateral agreement with an open source vendor. When customers balked at that, for reasons that will soon become clear, we realized that it would take more time to break through the years-long logjam of mutual suspicion and animosity between the open source world and Microsoft. "Project Summer" then, in effect, became "Project Next Summer" or perhaps "The Summer after That."

Less unclear, however, were the reasons why confidentiality was so important at this stage of the project. Foremost among these was the likelihood that if the small but politically potent minority within the open source community—led by "free software" icons Richard Stallman and Eben Moglen, the author of such trenchant works as "Anarchism Triumphant" and "The DotCommunist Manifesto"—learned of the project's existence, they would move quickly and decisively to scuttle any attempt at détente between the open source and proprietary software communities. That's because they saw the conflict between proprietary and open source software not as a market competition between two differing business models, software development approaches, and philosophical views of innovation. Rather, they viewed the open source and proprietary software divide as a moral and political war—as a fight between good and evil—in much the same way that old-time utopian socialists once viewed predatory capitalism. They opposed any sort of peaceful co-existence between the two software industry camps, let alone collaboration.

In this their attitude was strikingly reminiscent of that of the hard-core political ideologue once described by the historian Richard Hofstadter in his classic 1964 work, "The Paranoid Style in American Politics":

> *He does not see conflict as something to be mediated and compromised, in the manner of the working politician. Since what is at stake is always a conflict between absolute good and absolute evil, what is necessary is not compromise but the will to fight things out to a finish. This demand for total triumph leads to the formulation of hopelessly unrealistic goals, and since these goals are not even remotely attainable, failure constantly heightens [his] sense of frustration. Even partial success leaves him with the same feeling of powerlessness with which he began, and this in turn only strengthens his awareness of the vast and terrifying quality of the enemy he opposes.*

Customers, of course, viewed the situation very differently. Linux software, they felt, had clear advantages over Windows in certain areas; Windows had the advantage in others. But one thing was certain: Like smart chief information officers (CIOs) everywhere, they refused to be dependent on any one vendor for their data center needs. They ran—and would always continue to run—heterogeneous computer systems using both Linux and Windows. All they wanted was for Linux and Windows to work together more smoothly. They also wanted to stop worrying about the potential legal liabilities involved in using software that was the subject of IP disputes.

As a result, pressure had been mounting from large enterprise customers—everyone from Wal-Mart and AIG to Credit Suisse and the State of Delaware—for both sides of the open source versus proprietary software debate to get together and actually serve *their* needs instead of treating their differences like some sort of software holy war.

In short, customers wanted solutions, not excuses or rhetoric. And the only way for both sides to collaborate technically and actually produce these solutions was to create some sort of intellectual property bridge that respected both sides' innovations and intellectual property rights.

This was the backdrop to Ballmer's meeting with Susan Hauser. "Here's the problem," he told her that day in the closed conference room. "We want our intellectual property respected—we spend billions of dollars a year to create it—and Linux has made unauthorized use of our technology. We're also seeing that customers really want us to make Windows and Linux work together better. But we're not sure how to accomplish all this. We need to find a way to work things out with open source."

Hauser protested that she didn't know anything about intellectual property, but Ballmer dismissed that with a wave of his hand. "We don't need a patent lawyer for this job," he insisted. "What we need is someone who knows how to talk to customers—no, someone who knows how to *listen* to customers. Because we're going to need their help to solve this problem."

As events would soon demonstrate, Hauser became a key member of the IP&L team, with a finely-tuned ear for customer needs in the intellectual property arena. In the words of one customer, Susan was really the "Chief Listening Officer" for this project.

Two months after her talk with Ballmer, Hauser organized her first meeting in the sixth-floor Customer Briefing Center of Microsoft's New York offices. The CIOs of three Wall Street financial powerhouses were in attendance—even five years later, they ask that their identities not be revealed for fear that, as one put it, "some open source hacker might get pissed off and take down our whole network." The smells of a breakfast buffet filled the room, but no one was partaking of the food. They'd been asked to come to a confidential discussion of "intellectual property and open source issues"—a subject that made everyone in industry nervous—and their body language, Hauser recalls, was "tense in the extreme."

"I told them I wanted to be very candid with them," Hauser recalls, "and that I hoped they'd be candid with me. I told them that since we were now 'open for business' and willing to license our technology to everyone, it was time to address the intellectual property issues between proprietary and open source software companies. And then I said, 'Look, this is our problem, but it's kind of your problem, too. What should we do?'"

She felt the feedback she got indicated genuine empathy with Microsoft's challenge. They, too, had their own intellectual property that they wanted respected. Nonetheless, they didn't feel it made sense to enter any sort of direct IP licensing arrangement with Microsoft. "That's like getting in the middle of a war between France and Germany and signing a peace deal with only one party," said one of the CIOs in attendance. Besides, that wouldn't solve the interoperability problems. For that, Microsoft would have to engage in a long-term technical collaboration with one of the big Linux distributors, which they thought should probably be market leader Red Hat.

As another CIO put it: "Red Hat and Novell are businesses—publicly traded companies. Surely they'll see that working with you is good for customers—and thus good for them, too. We'll do our best to encourage all of you to work it out. But we can't get directly involved."

From July through September of 2004, Hauser met with dozens of large enterprises that had substantial investments in both Linux and Windows software. Everywhere she heard the same thing—strong support for Microsoft's initiative, a willingness to quietly encourage all the parties to negotiate, but an absolute refusal to become a party themselves to the negotiations.

It's worth noting here that even after all these meetings, not a word was ever leaked to the press or to anyone in the open source community about this highly sensitive Microsoft initiative. This was not only a testament to the trust and confidence that CIOs placed in Hauser. It was also critical to the eventual success of "Project Summer" itself.

The Cathedral and the Bazaar

Meanwhile, back in Redmond, my IP&L team was holding a marathon series of "Project Summer" meetings with

Microsoft's senior leadership to try to craft a strategic and tactical approach that would lead to a successful collaboration with an open source vendor. Conventional wisdom in the industry still held that there was an unbridgeable divide between the proprietary and open source sides of the industry. There were a number of reasons for this view. Partly it was because hard-core free software advocates opposed any real détente. But another reason was the basic structure of the industry itself.

Open source advocate Eric Raymond captured this structural divide in the title of his widely-read 1997 essay, "The Cathedral and the Bazaar." As Raymond noted, proprietary software was developed by companies that were well structured and organized, much like the designers and builders of a cathedral. Open source software, on the other hand, was created by a loosely connected community working across the Internet, more like the stereotypical Turkish Bazaar. When it came to patents, clearly the "cathedrals" of established companies could enter into licensing agreements with each other—they existed as legal corporate entities and usually had licensing offices. But it was far more difficult to conceive of a way for a "cathedral" to enter into a license agreement with a "bazaar," since the latter usually wasn't organized in a way to make this possible.

We spent a lot of time trying to figure out how to build a bridge between the "cathedral" and the "bazaar." We finally concluded that the core of a solution lay in the fact that, as the open source community had evolved, it had begun to sprout its own cathedrals existing right alongside the old community bazaar. Indeed, open source itself was becoming "big business." Not only had "pure" open source firms like Red Hat become significant commercial operations, but older established technology companies like IBM and Novell, which owned significant patent portfolios of their own, had also become major players in the development and for-profit commercialization of open source software.

Indeed, as Jonathan Corbet of the free software journal *LWN.Net* has noted, the Linux operating system itself today ironically owes more of its continuing development and evolution to corporate "cathedrals" than it does to the old "bazaar" hobbyists. Corbet's research found that at least 67 percent of new modifications to Linux are contributed by full-time corporate employees—and some analysts even say that figure has risen as high as 85 percent.

With commercial "cathedrals" now responsible for much of the development and distribution of open source software, therefore, it was becoming easier to contemplate the creation of a business framework and legal agreements that would enable some sort of patent and technology collaboration between Microsoft and an open source vendor, and would also protect open source developers still working in the "bazaar" from any concerns about patent liability.

Even so, there was still debate within Microsoft over whether or not such an overture was wise. Why not just beat them in the marketplace, some asked. Because, others replied, even apart from the market strength of open source software and the legitimacy in many situations of their mass-scale collective approach to software development, customers will always insist on maintaining heterogeneous systems in their data centers. In short, both Windows and Linux were here to stay, so we simply had better deal with that fact and figure out a way to work together.

As Ballmer himself said at the time, "Open source is not going away. Why should it?"

Peace or War?

Events in the broader technology community in mid–2004, meanwhile, were driving both sides toward some sort of catharsis—whether peace or war was not clear. The year before, a company called SCO Group had filed a number of lawsuits claiming that Linux was infringing SCO's copyrights, and that users and vendors of Linux should be held accountable. In response, Red Hat sued the SCO Group, seeking an injunction to stop its campaign against Linux as well as a declaratory judgment that Red Hat was not violating SCO's copyrights or trade secrets.

At the same time, Susan Hauser's customer contacts began making good on their promise to encourage both sides to avoid an intellectual property dispute and collaborate instead. Customer support for a Windows-Linux agreement was only heightened, of course, by developments in the *NTP v. RIM* patent infringement case, which by mid-2004 looked as if it were heading inexorably toward an injunction that would have shut down all of RIM's Blackberry handheld communicators in the United States. This would have disrupted corporate communications and, indeed, adversely affected the whole economy. Thus the possibility of litigation between Microsoft and Linux vendors was no longer simply a legal concern. It threatened the business continuity of corporate America itself.

Then, in July of 2004, the press began to speculate that Microsoft itself might sue Red Hat. The industry trade journal *eWeek* leaked an old internal 2002 Hewlett-Packard memo in which a senior HP official suggested that "Microsoft is about to launch legal action against the industry for shipping open source software that may force us out of using certain popular open source products." The basis for this executive's belief was never made clear. Perhaps it had something to do with past statements by Microsoft officials that had been (as Donald Rumsfeld might have put it) "unhelpful"—Steve Ballmer's 2001 off-the-cuff comment that Linux was a "cancer" comes to mind here. But whatever the source of the rumors, they were simply not true.

Interestingly, Red Hat Deputy General Counsel Mark Webbink also dismissed the memo as untrue. "Historically, Microsoft doesn't start lawsuits against competitors," he told *eWeek*. "They're not, despite what you might think, really that litigious a company."

Then Red Hat's Webbink made a statement to *eWeek* that was certainly not lost on the "Project Summer" team at Microsoft: "If Microsoft were to have such patents and start pursuing them, we'd be open to licensing such patented technologies, and I think Microsoft would be happy to license [them] to open source companies."

Bingo.

Soon after Webbink's remarks to *eWeek*, a major break-through occurred that transformed the vague hope of an open source–Microsoft rapprochement into a practical possibility. Confidentiality agreements signed by Microsoft strictly forbid me from disclosing any nonpublic information. But since the cat is out of the bag, as it were—and happily prancing about in the public square—I can refer the reader to the following press reports:

Red Hat's Mark Webbink confirmed in a May 28, 2007 interview in the industry trade publication *ITWire* that "Red Hat held talks with Microsoft." According to this report, "[Webbink] admitted that parlays had taken place over the last three years."

One month later, Red Hat's then-CEO Matthew Szulik himself corroborated Webbink's revelation that Microsoft and Red Had had engaged in substantive negotiations. In a widely read June 28, 2007 article, *Reuters* reported that Szulik confirmed that "[Red Hat] held talks with Microsoft over a patent agreement" aimed at enabling the two companies to resolve their differences and collaborate to improve the interoperability of Windows and Linux software.

What I can say is that Microsoft began its confidential negotiations with Red Hat in the fall of 2004 under Microsoft's internal code-name "Project Bridge Builder." And as I soon discovered, the challenges involved in trying to reach a working agreement between the open source and proprietary software worlds were among the most complex and difficult I had ever faced.

Consider, first of all, the philosophical question: How do you get your intellectual property respected by the other side when—not out of malice, but just as a matter of principle—they simply don't recognize the validity of your intellectual property? Open source companies like Red Hat and Novell certainly placed a high value on their own software copyrights and trademarks, but they truly believed that software patents shouldn't be legal and publicly opposed them. Our attitude, of course, was that it didn't matter whether or not they thought software patents should be legal: They *are* legal!

What's more, even if an open source company was willing to recognize and license patented software—as Mark Webbink said Red Hat was willing to do in his quote to *eWeek* in July of 2004—certain provisions of the open source general public license (GPL) under which open source companies distributed their products made such a license highly problematic. Section 7 of the GPL prohibited an open source vendor from entering into any royalty-bearing patent license that would constrain the further modification and redistribution of Microsoft's patented software code. In other words, once an open source company licensed our technology under the GPL, then anyone and everyone else in the world could use it or modify it at will—for free.

For obvious reasons, this was a problem for us. In traditional patent licensing, after all, the right to use a technology is granted only to the licensee, not to anyone else to whom the licensee may wish to offer it (unless the patent license explicitly allows for that). And we did not want to let everyone else in the world get a free ride on Microsoft's hard-earned and costly to develop R&D. Nonetheless, we saw the GPL license as a starting point for discussion, and hoped that we could ultimately find a way to make it work in a form that both sides could live with.

Then there was the business model hurdle. Even if an open source company recognized the validity—at least in theory—of Microsoft wanting to be compensated for the use of its patented software, they felt that because they didn't charge customers for their software, only for the service, how could they pay us for something their business model dictated should be free?

There was, in addition, a rather nontrivial mathematical problem: Even if an open source vendor agreed that our software patents were valid—and further, that they should be paid for—how much should they cost?

And finally, even if we somehow resolved all of the above issues, there were still a host of business and technical questions to grapple with—everything from how to collaborate in the marketing and sales of any new and more interoperable software products to how, given our very different software development methods, we could even design a technical collaboration that would enable us to jointly create those new and more interoperable products in the first place.

But there were also issues that, for lack of a better word, I have to call "political." For open source companies, these issues centered on their legitimate need to maintain the support of the open source community upon whom they relied for software development. For an open source firm to alienate these people would make no more sense than it would for Microsoft to alienate its developers. Thus any deal they concluded with Microsoft would have to be constructed and explained in a way that the "silent majority" of open source programmers could support.

To be sure, the hard-core free software advocates would probably never support a détente between the open source and proprietary software worlds, no matter how it was constructed. But that didn't mean it was wise for any open source company to incur their wrath unnecessarily.

Indeed, there is a story going around—perhaps apocryphal, but told to me by someone in a position to know—that illustrates precisely this point. It concerns the time that free software leader Richard Stallman once dragooned Red Hat into paying for a trip he wanted to make from his home in Boston to North Carolina, where Red Hat's headquarters is located, to visit an estranged girlfriend. He called a Red Hat executive and offered to give a speech to company employees in Raleigh in exchange for a plane ticket back home. (Stallman was once a self-described "squatter" on the MIT campus and apparently still eschews material wealth.) Rather than alienate Stallman and incur his wrath as well as that of his acolytes, this story goes, Red Hat had agreed. So after visiting his girlfriend, Stallman stopped by the company auditorium. There, dressed in his long white robe and foot-long beard—and wearing (I kid you not) a halo made out of a large old disk-drive platter—he gave a speech to about 200 Red Hat employees. Apparently, Stallman's speech was so filled with eye-glazing utopian visions of free software—of free *everything*, in fact, because Stallman believes that "all property is theft"—that by the end of his hour-long harangue only a handful of people were left in the room.

In any event, the reader will appreciate the extraordinary difficulty and sensitivity of the challenges Microsoft faced in its negotiations with Red Hat. But I have to give both Red Hat and Microsoft their due. Both sides put the right people into the negotiations—senior executives who understood the need for collaboration, as well as extremely bright legal, technical, and marketing experts—and both negotiating teams demonstrated time and again during the negotiations the mutual respect, sense of fair play, and willingness to compromise that this effort demanded.

Alas, after a year and a half of talks, Red Hat and Microsoft were unable to reach agreement. But we learned a great deal during the negotiations. Indeed, I was convinced that our experience with Red Hat had put us in a much better position to achieve success should another opportunity for talks with a major open source distributor ever arise.

A New Opening

In yet another of those remarkable synchronicities that mark this story, just such an opportunity did arise—shortly before the Red Hat negotiations finally collapsed. On June 2, 2006, Ron Hovsepian, the then-president and COO of Novell, called Microsoft COO Kevin Turner—while at IBM, Hovsepian had developed a close relationship with Turner when the latter was at Wal-Mart—and said he had heard that Microsoft was talking to other open source companies. Why not talk with Novell as well?

(Shortly afterwards, Hovsepian was named to replace Jack Messman as CEO after the Novell board ousted the latter for "failing to make big inroads against Linux market leader Red Hat," according to one news report.)

So a few days after that call to Kevin Turner, Brad Smith called Hovsepian back, and thus was born "Project Blue."

"One thing in particular that impressed me during our call was that it was apparent that Ron was prepared to be decisive and even bold," Brad recalls. "It was clear that he was going to drive a hard bargain, both for Novell as a company and for the interests of open source developers. But he was also prepared to help find a win-win solution. This level of decisiveness and commitment from a CEO was to my mind a missing ingredient that could help bring about an arrangement with an open source provider."

The first meeting with Novell was held on June 15, 2006, at the Chicago airport Hyatt. A convention of women body-builders was being held there at the same time, and it was a bit disconcerting to sit there trying to avoid any aggressive posturing by either side while through the window we could see a bevy of women bodybuilders flexing their muscles by the pool.

Although, in general, this and subsequent meetings were cordial and productive, there was a fair amount of bad blood between the two companies that we had to overcome.

"I attended the second meeting," recalls Susan Hauser, "and the atmosphere between the two sides was very icy at first—especially when the lawyers were talking." And no wonder. Under its previous CEO, Novell had brought two antitrust suits against Microsoft—the second one in November of 2004, during the very same week that we had paid out $536 million to settle Novell's first antitrust claim.

Nevertheless, says Hauser, "When we got to talking about the benefits of a Microsoft-Novell collaboration from the stand-point of customers, the mood improved dramatically. That's because it was pretty clear that those benefits would be substantial—as would the benefits to both of our businesses.

It was then that I realized that as long as we both kept our eyes on the prize—how working together would help customers—things would go pretty smoothly."

Now, it is usually the case in critical negotiations of this sort that when both parties have established a baseline level of trust, it is often a good idea to get the senior-most officials of both companies together to try to overcome major roadblocks barring the way forward in the negotiations. This can also be helpful because no effective collaboration can ever happen between firms without some level of trust and familiarity between the top executives who have the power to oversee it and commit the needed resources to it.

And here I want to emphasize a point I have made and will continue to make throughout this book: Corporations don't change their policies or make deals—people do. Whether we're talking about effecting cultural change within Microsoft, or Susan Hauser's enlistment of customers to encourage an accommodation between the proprietary and the open source world, or even the success of any collaboration with an open source vendor, it is human relations—the bonds of trust that individuals develop over time with each other—that are critical. Even when negotiations are ultimately unsuccessful—as was the case with Red Hat—these bonds of trust enable the parties to continue talking informally and perhaps come back together later on, when conditions might be more conducive to success.

Brad agreed that our two initial meetings with Novell had made enough progress that it made sense to arrange a higher-level get-together. On September 13, he outlined to the company's senior-most officials the general prospects for a deal with Novell. And the very next day, September 14, he and others held a face-to-face meeting in New York with Ron Hovsepian.

They met at 7:30 in the morning, with three parties on each side: Ron Hovsepian, Jeff Jaffe (the CTO), and General Counsel Joe LaSala for Novell; and Brad, Bob Muglia (the head of our server business), and Hank Vigil (who works on a number of key strategic relationships) for Microsoft. This was the first of what we would later call the "three-by-three" conversations.

They met at the midtown office of Microsoft's outside counsel, Covington & Burling—in the very same conference room, as it turned out, in which Microsoft had successfully negotiated its agreement with Sun Microsystems in March of 2004, which Hank Vigil and Brad had led. That prior negotiation had involved a substantial effort to overcome a decade's worth of mistrust as well as a rather large dose of creativity to bridge the gaps on some very complicated issues.

"Given the challenges of coming together with Novell," says Brad, "I thought it made sense to meet in the same conference room and use that as a symbol to underscore to both sides the need to work with the same degree of commitment and creativity. Plus, since the room had been lucky for us once before, I figured that couldn't hurt, either."

At the meeting, both sides agreed that any deal would have to provide a strong basis for sustained collaboration and not just a one-time signing event. In short, we needed to fundamentally re-orient the dynamic between our two companies if we wanted to achieve greater technical interoperability between our software products and put in place a patent pact. We'd need to take a creative approach to the patent issues, dealing with both the proprietary products of each company with a lump sum payment and also establishing a running royalty for open source code.

We didn't yet know what detailed elements this would require, but we realized that a successful deal would require three distinct but related agreements—one each for patent cooperation, technical collaboration, and business collaboration. To be sure, there were many complex issues that were going to require a lot of hard work. But at the same time, both sides felt that the gap between Microsoft and Novell could, in the end, be bridged.

"Done or Dead by Halloween"

As a forcing issue, Brad suggested a deadline of October 31 for reaching an agreement, and Ron agreed. This meant, if nothing else, that both sides needed to make these negotiations an absolute priority in terms of time and energy.

After the meeting, Brad called Steve Ballmer and walked him through the main points discussed. Ballmer supported the idea of an October 31 deadline—in fact, the two men talked about getting it "done or dead by Halloween." The point was to do everything we could to either reach an agreement, if that was possible, or walk away definitively and pursue other alternatives if it were not. But one thing we didn't want was a month-after-month discussion, with no end in sight. This partly reflected our experience in prior successful negotiations, such as the Toshiba deal (see Chapter 3), in which a deadline helped force matters to fruition.

The negotiators held a number of talks in early and mid-October. By then we had created two discrete teams at Microsoft, and Novell did the same. One team headed by Horacio Gutierrez and Anne Kelley led the patent negotiation. Horacio had by this time succeeded me as head of IP and Licensing—I had promised Bill and Brad when I was hired that I would serve in that position for three years, after which I would assume a non-managerial role as head of IP Policy and Strategy—and was a strong advocate of the company's efforts to deploy intellectual property as a bridge to collaboration. Anne, meanwhile, had become head of the IP licensing function following her success in the Toshiba negotiations.

As for the business and technical collaboration negotiations, these were led by Hossein Nowbar, the senior lawyer for our server business. Hossein's team included technical and marketing personnel from our server business, and they worked closely with Bob Muglia on defining the interoperability and other business collaboration steps we would recommend.

The teams did a lot of work by e-mail and over the phone, and the patent teams from the two companies met in person in San Francisco on October 11. The three-by-three group—Ron Hovsepian, Jeff Jaffe, and Joe LaSala for Novell, and Brad Smith, Bob Muglia, and Hank Vigil for Microsoft—talked together regularly by phone to take stock of progress, address issues that were escalated up from the negotiators, and work directly on the economic aspects and the financial commitments for each company. Nevertheless, we still remained open to possible arrangements with other open source providers and were prepared to close a deal with someone else if that appeared to make more sense or the Novell talks collapsed.

By mid–October, the teams had made good progress. We had hammered out a plan to create a joint research facility staffed by employees from both companies. This would be the focal point for our new technical collaboration on the key interoperability demands of customers regarding virtualization, web services management, and document format compatibility.

On the patent front, the teams agreed to a general approach under which Novell would pay a running royalty to Microsoft for revenue generated by the distribution of its SUSE Linux subscriptions, and we would make an investment to resell some of these subscriptions, because at least initially these would be the only Linux subscriptions that respected Microsoft's patents. We also agreed to form a sales team under Susan Hauser to focus on this resale opportunity.

Despite this progress, a significant number of open issues remained and even by the third week of October, the finish line still seemed far away. The question now was, How do we move quickly so we can close a deal by Halloween?

We decided to get the two negotiating teams together the following week to basically work around the clock. The longest and most complicated list of open issues, of course, was on the patent side, so Ron Hovsepian asked Joe LaSala and Jeff Jaffe to come to Redmond and work more closely with us to see if the patent issues could be resolved.

Brad arranged to meet personally with Joe and Jeff on October 27. So on the 26th, Microsoft's patent team met with Brad to prepare him for the next day's meeting. They had prepared a patent agreement term sheet that listed twelve open issues, but some of them had as many as four or five sub-parts.

"I felt like I was cramming for a law school exam," Brad laughs, "and yet at the same time I had to probe the team regarding areas of possible compromise. We had some pretty frank discussions about the difference between negotiating and debating, because I was going to need to do the former and not just explain to Novell why we thought our positions were sound."

By the conclusion of the meeting on the 27th, substantial progress had been made and Brad felt that things looked promising. He, together with Joe and Jeff, then spoke with Novell's CEO by phone, and they all agreed that each side would try its best to reach agreement in time to announce it in San Francisco the following Thursday, November 2. Ron said he would come to Redmond on Wednesday, November 1, for a meeting with Steve Ballmer to make the final press conference arrangements.

By Monday morning, October 30, everyone was basically in work-around-the-clock mode. The patent teams from the two companies were working out of conference rooms at the Bellevue Hyatt. The business and technical collaboration team was camped out in a conference room on the fifth floor of Building 34, just around the corner from Brad's conference room.

On many issues, progress was steady but slow. But new problems kept emerging. Some of these focused on the technical collaboration. But the most difficult, as expected, centered on the patent issues, and Gutierrez saw how crucial it was to keep the negotiating team focused on the broader strategic benefits to be gained by concluding an agreement with Novell.

"On several occasions when things got bogged down in lawyerly details, I had to pull the team out of the meetings to remind them what our main objective was," Gutierrez recalls. "We couldn't let our concerns about legal risk stand in the way of this new opportunity."

That people in Microsoft should still be struggling, even unconsciously, with the need for collaboration with open source is hardly surprising. That's how change happens—in fits and starts, and only over time. And the continuing pull of Microsoft's old "man the barricades" attitude did not just afflict members of the negotiating team. During this period, I was still occasionally receiving what I began to call my "Sunday night e-mails from Bill" in which the chairman worried that I was "killing his business!" As usual, this was Bill's way of testing the degree to which we had really thought through our planned course of action and its future implications. But perhaps it also suggested that old defensive habits take time to fade, even among senior leaders such as Gates who were sincerely committed to our new direction.

A Hitch Develops

On Monday, October 30th, a hitch developed. The Novell team told us that they had concluded that the open source royalty plan would not comply with their obligations under the general public license (GPL). The fundamental problem was that the GPL prohibited Novell from paying Microsoft an ongoing royalty for a direct patent license to cover Linux. In effect, this was a poison pill designed by hard-core free software advocates who wanted to prevent commercial collaboration that involved ongoing economic commitments between open source and proprietary software companies.

On the other hand, if Microsoft had agreed to a license from Novell that was fully paid up for a fixed sum, this would have translated under the GPL to convey the same patent rights to every other distributor and user of Linux as well. It would have meant that Novell in effect would have had to pay up front not only for itself but for its competitors and the entire industry as well. It would have also meant that Microsoft would have had to accept a one-time payment without any effective ability to estimate the volume of distribution that would be implicated.

This was a roadblock that threatened to halt the whole deal.

"Some of our people felt that we could not do a deal under the GPL terms," Gutierrez concedes. "But we kept trying—we really tried—to understand Novell's situation. They are a leader in the open source community, and they couldn't sign a deal that really went against the basic licensing rules of that community."

Gutierrez pauses a moment. "So we tried to think outside the box. How could we do this so that neither side had to violate its principles? And then it hit us—let's just make an end run around the distributor licensing impasse and focus instead directly on the customer!"

118

Microsoft's team, it seems, had finally concluded after a great deal of out-of-the-box brainstorming that while the GPL precluded a direct patent license involving a running royalty between Microsoft and Novell, there was nothing in it that prevented Novell from paying to Microsoft a running royalty for a covenant-not-to-sue that Microsoft provided directly to Novell's customers. In other words, from a legal perspective this new patent covenant would never run through Novell at all, so it would not run afoul of the GPL. It was this creative stroke of genius, which emerged only in the final hours of negotiations, that in my opinion really made the breakthrough with Novell possible.

It was also the best of all possible solutions for customers. Instead of worrying whether either side had secured a valid patent license that could survive any later legal disputes, the covenant-not-to-sue completely absolved them of any IP concerns at all.

On Monday evening, October 30th, Anne Kelley walked the Novell team through our proposed new approach. They listened and agreed to think about it overnight. The next morning, the 31st, the two teams reconvened separately at 9.00 A.M. The Novell team consulted among themselves and with their outside counsel, while our side waited nervously in another room—which felt a bit like waiting for a jury to finish its deliberations.

At 12:15 P.M., the two teams met together and the Novell team announced their verdict: the new approach, they said, would indeed work under the GPL. Things were back on track!

But there was one other new wrinkle. Novell wanted us to go farther in terms of offering a commitment that we would not sue individual open source developers for patent infringement. We previously had agreed that we would not bring patent infringement litigation against open source developers who were "hobbyists"—individuals who write code not with the expectation of making money, but because they enjoy solving technical challenges and participating in a community of enthusiasts who recognize and encourage one another's talents.

Now Novell wanted us to go farther. They wanted us to create a second commitment that would protect open source developers who contribute code to OpenSUSE.org, the vehicle that Novell used to collect the code for its version of Linux. Ron Hovsepian had decided that he wouldn't sign an agreement unless we offered this to the open source community.

It was a bit of a Halloween surprise. But after thinking about it that afternoon, we decided that the request was reasonable and we should run it by Bill Gates. As it happened, Brad ran into Bill in the hallway—Bill was guiding his costumed son down the decorated hallways of Building 34, trick-or-treating—and Bill agreed that it made sense to accede to Novell's request.

The next day, November 1, Ron and the entire Novell executive team came to Redmond. Together with Brad, they met with Steve Ballmer in his conference room to go through the final plans for the press conference the next day. We had public statements of support from top executives at Intel, AMD, HP, Dell, SAP, and many other firms. Major customers like Goldman Sachs and Hewlett-Packard had also agreed to send senior executives to participate in the press conference.

The only problem was that the agreements were still not finished. While the top tier of issues was now complete, there was still quite a lot of devil left in the details. So Brad met again with Ron, Jeff, and Joe from Novell and worked through a list of 18 remaining unresolved issues that had escalated up from the three agreements. They resolved every item in only 90 minutes—even to the point of trading one company's position on one issue for the other company's position on another.

Reflecting on this horse-trading, Brad noted that, "There's always a risk that those in the trenches will come to hold a position so intensely that they won't let go of it, even when the greater good and opportunity requires it. But everyone understood that compromise was required to reach our goal, and everyone was extremely professional and collegial in working together. We would debate what to do, but once a decision was made, we all moved forward to execute it. That was a very important part of what made the teams on both sides so successful."

As it turned out, of course, there were still more details to address—aren't there always?—and work continued on through the night and into the day of the press conference itself. But at 11:00 A.M., the Microsoft group, including Steve Ballmer, took off from Boeing Field in Seattle and landed at the San Francisco International Airport at about 1:00 P.M., giving us only an hour before the 2:00 P.M. press conference commenced.

The first thing they learned upon landing was that the news had started to leak, and Novell's stock price had shot up 15 percent in the final hour of trading that day. As Brad and Steve climbed into a Ford Explorer for the drive into San Francisco, Brad called Redmond, hoping to get the news that all of the agreements were now ready for signature. Instead Hossein Nowbar reported that the teams were still working through some details.

"I tried to project calmness, while Steve kept asking me how it was that the lawyers were still not finished," Brad laughs.

The press was already filing into the press conference room when Brad and Steve arrived at 1:40 P.M. They shook hands with Ron, Jeff, Joe, and the others from Novell who had also just arrived. Everyone wondered what was happening in Redmond in the negotiating rooms, but no one seemed to have a good answer. At 10 minutes to 2:00 P.M., someone asked whether we should start the press conference without signed agreements. We decided we should not.

Instead, Brad and Joe LaSala took the elevator down two floors to a room full of PR personnel from the two companies and our respective agencies, their laptops and printers humming. Both men got on the phone to their respective teams and begged them to please finish the last details and e-mail the agreements for the two of them to sign.

Horacio Gutierrez and the patent team proudly crossed the finish line first, at 1:58 P.M.—two minutes before the deadline. Brad remained on the phone with Hossein, meanwhile, who insisted that his people were just proofreading the last changes in the agreement.

"I remember I looked at my watch and saw it was 2:00 P.M.," says Brad. "So I pleaded with him to proofread the thing faster! A few minutes later—just past the deadline—the agreements finally came off the printer."

Brad and Joe each started furiously signing the documents.

"But then all of a sudden my pen ran out of ink," Brad sighs. "Unbelievable! So I reached over to a whiteboard and finished signing with a magic marker."

Brad and Joe then dashed back upstairs, where they and the other executives hustled out on stage to announce the world's first business, legal, and technical cooperation agreement between a proprietary and open source software company.

"Make This Work!"

"They said it couldn't be done," declared Steve Ballmer. "This is a new model of cooperation and a true evolution of Microsoft's relationship with the industry."

And indeed, few had believed it would ever be possible to bridge the gap between the proprietary and open source software worlds—a philosophical divide that goes back 30 years to open source's origins in the academic UNIX environment. But a funny thing happened on the way to the software Tower of Babel: the customer made his voice heard. He wanted Windows and Linux to work together seamlessly and efficiently, and he needed assurance that in using these two products he was not going to be violating anyone's intellectual property rights.

Novell's CEO Ron Hovsepian also spoke at the press conference. "When I first reached out to Steve and Microsoft," he noted, "it was a conversation about how to work together with our customers. Now, I haven't had a lot of opportunities to work that closely with Steve and his team, and they may get painted with a certain brush at times"—perhaps Ron was alluding here to Ballmer's infamous 2001 "Linux is a cancer" quote—"but I will tell you that at a personal level I've been very impressed with the integrity and the approach they took to creating this working relationship, and the deep commitment they have shown to us at Novell in making this relationship a reality."

To many in the audience, the announcement seemed to offer all the hope and promise of a Camp David Accord for the information technology industry. Indeed, statements of support poured in from a wide range of companies and industry analysts. But given the fate of many past industry "alliances," it was hardly surprising that some in the audience wondered whether this would turn out to be just another dog-and-pony show—a lot of PR puffery and not much else.

Susan Hauser was at the press conference, though, and she had no doubts about how seriously Microsoft viewed the deal. "Everyone was applauding, the cameras were flashing, and then Steve took my arm and pulled me aside," she recalls. "He looked down at me—he's a big guy—and with this really intense look on his face he whispered three words: 'Make this work!' "

Which is exactly what she and her counterparts dedicated the next two years of their lives to doing. Hauser worked with Novell's Susan Heystee and the other members of both teams to organize a disciplined process for not only solving the technical interoperability issues between Linux and Windows, but for building and sustaining a joint marketing and sales effort between the two firms as well. Weekly and monthly meetings, spreadsheets of tasks and duties set against timelines for completion, rapid intervention whenever problems developed, and the commitment by senior executives at both firms to provide the resources and staff needed to accomplish the mission—these are the hallmarks of any successful collaboration.

"In my opinion," says Gutierrez, "Susan has done a marvelous job. She made this work."

The ultimate test of any collaboration, of course, is its effect upon the businesses of each partner. And here the results have been clear. During just the first year of the agreement, Novell's paid Linux subscription growth rate jumped from under 2 percent in 2006 to nearly 39 percent in 2007—the highest growth rate in the industry! Novell also increased its market share by 3 percent, compared to a market share decline of 2 percent for competitor Red Hat.

As market researcher IDC noted: "Novell's revenue jumped dramatically in 2007—thanks to the company's partnership and interoperability efforts with Microsoft."

What's more, given that many Red Hat customers are on three-year contracts, those figures are probably lagging indicators of the full extent to which the Microsoft deal will help Novell's business. Once those contracts expire, industry analysts say, we can expect to see even more customers switch to Novell from Red Hat, since the latter cannot provide either the IP assurance or the improvements in Linux-Windows interoperability that Novell can.

The deal has also been good for Microsoft. By resolving some of the customer's greatest Windows and Linux interoperability problems—the core benefit to Microsoft from the agreement—it resulted in an increase in Microsoft's own business as a result.

In fact, the deal proved to be so beneficial to both companies that in November of 2008—two years after the collaboration was first launched—Microsoft and Novell announced a major additional investment of up to $100 million in their collaboration to meet increased customer demand for our more integrated Linux and Windows platforms. This new investment will provide new tools, training, and resources to enterprise customers.

In the end, the Microsoft-Novell deal resulted in one of the greatest advances in the interoperability of large enterprise software ever, and helped to unleash a flurry of new patent and technical collaboration deals between Microsoft and open source companies. Among the most significant were our collaborations with the Korean giants Samsung and LG Electronics, Fuji-Xerox, and with Linux distributors Xandros, Linspire (now combined), and TurboLinux. The Samsung deal represented an important collaboration with major consumer electronics company involving both hardware and software IP, including Linux. It also led to a technology collaboration in a new line of networked digital photo-frames sold under the Samsung brand. The Linux distributor deals, meanwhile, enhanced the whole ecosystem of Windows and Linux cross-platform products.

The Die-Hards React

To no one's surprise, of course, the die-hards in the open source movement have not been pleased with the deal. A boycott of Novell was organized by opposition elements, but this seems to have had no effect on Novell's business—proving once again that the majority of open source developers simply want to create good software and serve customers, not wage software jihad.

Yet despite the demonstrated benefits to customers from the Microsoft-Novell deal, there are those within the community who continue to argue that while the improved interoperability of Linux and Windows that resulted from the collaboration may have been beneficial, the need for customer IP assurance was never anything more than a red herring designed to foster "FUD" (fear, uncertainty, and doubt) within the open source community.

"Getting Linux and Windows to work better together makes good, hard business sense," wrote blogger Steven J. Vaughan-Nichols in the August 22, 2008 edition of the trade publication *Computerworld*, "[and] there are many good reasons to buy into Novell-Microsoft. [But] IP protection from Microsoft isn't one of them." In fact, claimed the blogger, "I talk to a lot of business people who have already committed themselves or are considering using Linux in their data-centers and offices. Not one of them is seriously concerned about Linux's IP issues."

Really?

Leave aside for a moment Vaughan-Nichols's apparent amnesia for the widespread fear that just two years earlier had rippled through the nation's large data centers over the NTP-RIM patent suit's threat to Blackberry communications. Forget also about the customer fears widely reported in the media during the SCO-Red Hat litigation. Vaughan-Nichols's statement simply boggles the mind. Indeed, one has to ask: To whom has he been talking—or rather, *not* talking?

Consider, for example, the following published comments from major Linux customers.

"At Nationwide, it is important to us that our software is compliant with all IP licensing requirements," said David Zelle, director of systems engineering and administration at the lender. "We are actively looking to migrate to [Novell's] Linux versus other brands of Linux."

Added Nancy Stewart, Wal-Mart's CTO at the time: "We have wanted information technology vendors to deliver interoperability and IP assurance between multiple platforms for some time now. We are pleased that Microsoft and Novell are fulfilling that need."

Then there was this comment from Eugene Roman, group president for systems and technologies at Bell Canada: "This agreement is a positive example of how companies with different business models and approaches to intellectual property can work together. Hopefully this is a model that others in the industry will repeat."

Meanwhile, Jonathan Zuck, president of the Association for Competitive Technologies, had this to say: "Microsoft and Novell should be commended for putting customers and innovation before ideology. This is the kind of achievement that can only be reached when parties respect one another's innovations and intellectual property and put their customers first."

And Mark Popolano, until recently the global chief information officer for insurance giant AIG, said simply: "Microsoft and Novell's commitment to working together to deliver interoperability and IP assurance helps us achieve [our] mission."

And finally, here's what the community's own Open Source Development Labs had to say: "We are glad to see these two companies collaborating to further diminish the legal threat posed to developers and customers by patent assertions," declared CEO Stuart Cohen. "This is good for customer confidence in Linux, the open source community, and the IT ecosystem."

In the end, there were many ironies in this story. The first, of course, is that while the negotiations involved quite possibly the most complex area in all of law and business, they were resolved successfully only when our highly-trained IP lawyers worked together with individuals who had a broad range of business and strategic skills.

And therein lies a lesson that IP managers throughout corporate America would do well to keep in mind: No corporate IP department can consist of only IP attorneys and expect to be successful in endeavors such as licensing, dispute resolution, and value creation that require a more liberal range of business, marketing, and communications skills.

It is also ironic that while the Microsoft–Novell rapprochement was clearly the result of the good faith and determination of senior executives of both companies, it was in truth even more forcefully propelled to success by the voice of the customer itself.

Indeed, so valuable was the feedback that Susan Hauser obtained in 2004 from enterprise customers on the need for Linux and Windows interoperability that Microsoft later launched an Interoperability Executive Customer Council (IECC)—headed by Hauser—to provide a forum where the voice of the customer could be heard and acted upon in all areas of our business.

But the most striking irony of all is that while intellectual property started out as the central bone of contention between Microsoft and the open source world, in the end it supplied the essential alchemy that transformed both sides from enemies into friends.

A Distinction without (Much) Difference

So whither the future of open source and proprietary software?

The former CEO of Open Source Development Labs, Stuart Cohen, proclaimed in a December 1, 2008 article in *BusinessWeek* that "the open source model is broken." By this he meant that open source companies who hoped to make money from their free software by charging customers for support and add-on features "have failed or will falter, and their ranks may swell as the economy worsens." This requires a new mindset, he argued, which sees open source more as a means than an end in itself.

But the larger issue may be that the distinction between open source and proprietary software itself—a largely ideological and extremely emotional distinction—has rapidly begun to lose its meaning as companies on both sides of the former divide increasingly develop "mixed source" solutions. Many open source companies today are adding proprietary offerings to their products to differentiate these from competitors. At the same time, proprietary software firms like Microsoft are now participating in open source development projects, and in our own case, even shipping open source code in products. The most successful software solutions of tomorrow will likely be a hybrid in which the old open source versus proprietary software conflict plays little if any role.

And as for Microsoft's future relations with Red Hat?

Certainly the open source leader has seen the benefits that Novell's collaboration with Microsoft has yielded over the past two-and-a-half years—not only to its arch competitor, Novell, but to large enterprise customers as well. Then, too, as reported in Peter Galli's blog *Platform Dive*, "There can be little doubt that Red Hat is worried about the loss of some business from a number of large enterprises who are enthusiastic about the technical cooperation and patent indemnification agreement signed by Microsoft and Novell last year."

Given all this—not to mention all the good will developed by the Red Hat and Microsoft negotiating teams over the course of 18 months—might we someday see a renewed attempt at a rapprochement between the two companies?

Let's just say I wouldn't be surprised if we did.

Chapter 5

Leadership Starts at the Top

O n February 3, 1976, a then–20-year-old Bill Gates wrote an "Open Letter" that, more than any other single act of the Microsoft founder and chairman, illuminated his singular vision of the role that intellectual property would play in the creation of a software industry that has today become one of the most powerful engines of the world economy.

The letter was addressed to the Homebrew Computer Club, an organization of hobbyists that had formed one year earlier in Silicon Valley following the introduction of the world's first personal computer, the Altair 8800, which was sold as a mail-order kit through advertisements in *Popular Electronics* and other hobbyist magazines. Gates at that time was running a small firm with his old high-school classmate Paul Allen in Albuquerque, New Mexico, and according to Gates, the moment he and Allen saw the ad for the Altair kit computer in *Popular Electronics*, they realized that the price of personal computers would likely drop to the point where they could become ubiquitous in society. If so, this would create a lucrative new business opportunity in selling the software that could transform such devices from hobbyist toys into powerful communications and productivity tools for consumers and businesses alike. So Gates and Allen designed a version of the BASIC programming language to run on the Altair.

The problem was, most computer hobbyists at the time saw software as the inseparable (yet separately valueless) complement to computer hardware—the "mayonnaise on the sandwich," in Nathan Myhrvold's memorable phrase. "You wouldn't eat a bowl of mayonnaise by itself," says Myhrvold of the attitude towards software at that time, "and you wouldn't pay extra to have it put on the sandwich." And so most computer users simply passed around for free the software that Gates's firm, then called Micro-soft (with a hyphen), had developed.

In his letter, Gates drove a very sharp stake in the ground—a stake that would later serve as a key pillar of the most powerful wealth-creating industry on earth.

"To me, the most critical thing in the hobby market right now is the lack of good software," he wrote. "The feedback we have gotten from the hundreds of people who say they are using BASIC has all been positive. Two surprising things are apparent, however: (1) Most of these users never bought BASIC, and (2) the amount of royalties we have received from sales to hobbyists makes the time [we] spent on Altair BASIC worth less than $2 an hour."

Apparently, wrote Gates, the prevailing assumption among computer users is that "hardware must be paid for, but software is something to share." This attitude, he insisted, "prevents good software from being written. Who can afford to do professional work for nothing? [Who] can put three man-years into programming, finding all bugs, documenting his product and distribute for free?"

In other words, if the world wanted good software, it had to be treated as valuable and paid for, and the intellectual property embodied in it respected.

Then, in an astonishingly modest proposal, Gates wrote: "Nothing would please me more than being able to hire ten programmers and deluge the market with good software."

Which, of course, is exactly what he did—first ten programmers, then a thousand, then ten thousand, until today the commercial software industry that Gates helped create now employs 18 million people worldwide, nearly 80 percent of them working in some way with Microsoft software.

Back in 1976, Gates's argument was a controversial if not unpopular one, and his "Open Letter" was roundly criticized. But what some people mistook for avarice was actually vision. Among the architects of the Digital Revolution, Bill was one of only a relative few who understood not only the importance of intellectual property to software development, but the defining role that software as an independent force would play in the emerging knowledge economy. Indeed, even a decade after that letter, most high-tech leaders still had trouble believing that software by itself was valuable or that it could be a driving force in global economic growth.

Again, here is Nathan Myhrvold, the former head of Microsoft's research organization and later the founder and chairman of Intellectual Ventures, an invention and patent licensing firm: "It sounds crazy now, but back in those days it was not a foregone conclusion that a software company was a good thing. I remember at the Agenda Conference in the mid-1980s, a very prestigious high-tech industry event, there was a panel discussion called, 'Can Microsoft Make It Without Hardware?' I mean, people still weren't sure software was valuable apart from hardware."

Myhrvold had founded his own startup software company earlier in the 1980s before selling it to Microsoft and going to work for Gates, and he remembers how difficult it was to sell his product. "I went to Hewlett-Packard with our software, but they told me they'd only pay me a small fixed fee for it rather than a per-copy royalty. The guy I was meeting with said, 'C'mon, you're asking me to pay as much for your software as I pay for the capacitors in my power supply?' And I said, 'Damn right, because my software makes your computer usable and salable, whereas no one gives a crap about your capacitors!' So that's the kind of old-fashioned thinking that Bill was challenging back then. And the world is hugely better off for his having done so."

Gates's Unusual Role

I have often told people that in my 30-plus years in business, I have never met a single CEO or chairman who is as intimately involved in intellectual property strategy as Bill Gates. At first, I had assumed that this was due to quirks in Gates's personality. As Bill himself told me, "My dad was a lawyer, and so I guess I've always had an interest in legal-related issues. And then also the complexities of the intellectual property system have always fascinated me."

But not until I learned the history of Bill's "Open Letter" did I understand the real reason for his close involvement in IP matters. From his first days as a programmer, Bill had an almost prophetic understanding that the defense of software creators' intellectual property rights was the crucible in which a new, world-changing industry could be forged. And this "IP awareness," if that's the right term, has infused every aspect of his leadership of Microsoft over the years.

Indeed, it was precisely Gates's insistence on retaining the copyright to the version of DOS he developed for IBM's personal computer in 1981 that enabled Microsoft, once millions of IBM clones flooded the market, to become the dominant force in PC software and eventually the world's biggest software company.

"What was at first just an intuitive sense on Bill's part that quality software would flood the market if developers were allowed to reap the rewards of their investment later became a fundamental principle of the new software industry," says Microsoft's Vice President of IP and Licensing Horacio Gutierrez. "No one really grasped the truth of that principle before he came along, nor defended it more passionately."

Adds Ken Lustig, who as the company's general manager of IP acquisitions and investments, has worked closely with Gates: "At every critical juncture faced by this company, Bill has shown incredible foresight into the interplay between intellectual property, finance, and business strategy. Whether it was retaining the rights to MS-DOS in the 1981 IBM deal, or licensing technologies from Xerox's PARC [Palo Alto Research Center] that we were going to need for the Windows interface, or investing in firms that had IP rights we wanted, Bill is the smartest guy in the room when it comes to IP. Which is pretty incredible, when you consider that he is also overseeing one of the world's most complex and competitive businesses. And that level of IP intelligence is just not common in most executive suites."

Indeed, what other chairman or CEO conducts regular patent reviews with senior staff to discuss the firm's IP assets and patenting efforts—and comes to such meetings armed with a fluent understanding of everything from the competitive landscape of patenting in the industry to key patent numbers and claims language? What other senior corporate leader takes such a hands-on role in the utilization of IP assets in financial and market strategy? And what other top executive meets regularly with a cross-disciplinary team of technologists, IP attorneys and business strategists to conduct "forward invention" sessions that try to anticipate the direction of innovation not just in the current or the next product cycle, but 10 years in the future?

Ten years in the future? Many CEOs today are hard-pressed to devote any time or thought to anything but the next quarterly earnings report!

Even seemingly small details don't escape Gates's notice. Consider the following e-mail, which Gates sent to the Business Leadership Team, composed of senior executives and business group leaders at Microsoft, on April 28, 2004, just 10 months after I started working at Microsoft:

> *I did my yearly review of the IP group yesterday. We had a goal of filing 2000 patents this fiscal year and will end up filing 2128. This is very impressive. This is a huge increase and a huge investment for everyone involved but very important for the company. The issue rate lags the filing rate by about four years but Marshall has some ideas about getting that to move up faster as well.*

For Bill, of course, it was not just about the numbers, but also about the quality of the patents and what the numbers suggested about the organization's embrace of IP's importance. "I was very impressed with the relationship between the product groups and the IP group," he went on to say in his e-mail, referring to the embedding of senior patent lawyers in the business units that we initiated the previous year in order to raise the strategic quality of our patents and enhance the business opportunities made available by a higher-quality IP portfolio. "The collaboration around setting patent goals and achieving them is very good."

Now, I can guess what you, the reader, is thinking right now: Sure, Bill Gates's close involvement in IP matters is all very interesting, but is this sort of top executive participation really necessary? If a company has a competent general counsel and chief patent counsel, and a well-functioning IP organization, should the CEO or chairman really burden himself with matters that most people find to be the most complex and esoteric in all of law and business?

Well, let me think about that. . . . *Yes!*

Corporate America's Dirty Little Secret

After all, intellectual property has now become the chief source of wealth of the modern corporation. IP and other intangible assets today account for upwards of 80 percent of the market capitalization of all public companies in the world—with brands, copyrights, patents, and technological know-how now comprising the lion's share of these intangibles. On the face of it, therefore, managing such assets would appear to offer CEOs their single greatest opportunity for maximizing firm value—this task being, of course, the chief responsibility of any CEO.

As Nir Kossovsky and Jorge M. Torres of the Intangible Asset Finance Society report, "Our data consistently show that superior stewards of intangible assets reward their shareholders with returns that are on the order of three times greater than their peers."

And yet—and let's just be honest here—the dirty little secret of corporate governance today is that the overwhelming majority of CEOs, chairmen, and corporate board members devote literally zero thought and effort to the management of their firms' intellectual property assets. Indeed, few even have any idea what's in their IP portfolio, let alone what to do with it. And so responsibility for intellectual property management is usually left to the corporate legal office and is regarded merely as a "rights" issue rather than a business imperative deserving of attention from top executives responsible for the firm's strategic and commercial growth.

Can you imagine the commanding general of an army not knowing how to deploy 80 percent of his military assets to achieve his objectives—not even knowing, in fact, what those assets are—and instead leaving that task solely to a staff officer? I daresay any such general would be relieved of his command. Yet that's pretty much the situation today in executive suites all across corporate America with regard to intellectual assets. In my view, this is nothing but an invitation to shareholder lawsuits over mismanagement of firm IP assets.

Says Nathan Myhrvold: "The average grade for the executive management of patents today is probably a D-minus. Most patents are not managed at all; they just sit there."

Indeed, a study by BTG International several years ago found that two-thirds of all U.S. firms have patent assets that they fail to exploit. The value of those neglected assets? According to *Forbes:* "U.S. companies are wasting $1 *trillion* a year by not capitalizing on their patents."

This is not to say, of course, that C-level executives are completely unaware of IP's importance to firm success. Over the last decade, a number of developments spurred CEOs and other senior executives to acquire at least a modest respect for the defining role that IP can often play in a company's fortunes. Among these was a spate of high profile, multi-hundred-million-dollar patent infringement awards—serious money even to a large corporation. Also important was the publication in 2000 of my co-author's influential *Rembrandts in the Attic*, a book that *Forbes* magazine noted had "captured the attention of the business community." In the words of *Intellectual Asset Management* magazine, the leading publication in the IP field: "No book has had more impact on corporate IP management than *Rembrandts*. It helped take IP out of the labs and the lawyers' offices and into the very center of corporate decision-making."

But, unfortunately, corporate America's new understanding of IP's importance is still largely confined to the realm of rhetoric, not practical leadership.

Says Fujitsu's former VP of IP, Masanobu Katoh: "Corporate leadership has finally come to understand the importance of intellectual property to firm success—but only at the level of theory. They can recite the rhetoric about 'aligning IP with business strategy' and 'using IP to build the business.' But how, exactly, to do this? We are not so good at this yet."

Indeed, in 2004 the consulting firm Accenture commissioned a study conducted by the Economist Intelligence Unit that found that 78 percent of senior executives believed that "managing intellectual capital is an important management issue." Yet 95 percent of those same executives said that their companies failed to manage IP assets effectively—with 33 percent saying their companies made no systematic effort to do so at all.

Or as *Forbes* magazine once put it: "A lot of CEOs talk about patent strategy, but nothing really happens because [they and their] internal organization simply don't know how to do it."

Why the CEO Disconnect?

Several factors account for this rather striking disconnect between the enormous value of intellectual property and the minimal involvement of CEOs in its utilization. Consider, first of all, that most of today's senior corporate leaders were educated and came of age during the 1970s and 1980s, when tangible assets like plant and equipment still comprised roughly 80 percent of the market value of public companies. If their educators, bosses, and mentors ever spoke of intellectual property at all—and that's doubtful—it was probably just to caution them about the need for a good legal department to manage the risks associated with IP. But as the economy shifted from an industrial to a knowledge base over the last 30 years and IP was transformed from a legal instrument into a strategic business asset, these executives were left unprepared.

Indeed, when you consider that IP assets have only been widely recognized as a strategic asset in business for the last 10 to 15 years, it's hardly a surprise that intellectual property is still typically excluded from the strategy processes of most firms today. CEOs and other senior executives have had more than a century of experience to inform their management of R&D, sales, operations, and other strategic activities. But when it comes to intellectual property, there is very little legacy knowledge or experience for top leaders to draw upon in managing this new asset class—either within the business units, corporate-wide, or in relations with outside firms. And even today there is still almost nothing in the way of professional literature or pedagogy that integrates IP management into the broader array of managerial skills taught in business school.

Another source of CEO myopia regarding intellectual property is the fact that IP assets, despite being the chief form of corporate wealth, actually never show up on the balance sheet, thanks to a centuries-old accounting system that was designed for a world in which tangible assets were the only assets worth valuing. And since, as the saying goes, "You can't manage what you can't measure," CEOs can perhaps be excused for focusing on the all-mighty quarterly report and neglecting IP opportunities that are invisible to the balance sheet.

"IP value typically escapes the balance sheet," writes Bruce Berman in *Intellectual Asset Management*. Which is why, in the rare cases when CEOs have shown any enthusiasm at all for IP, it has usually been only for the royalty-generating potential of patent licensing. As Berman notes: "Revenues from patent licenses are attractive to [CEOs] because they are easily understood. But royalty generation is [only] one of the many ways intellectual assets can be monetized. It is not the definitive way. Many companies under pressure to perform get sucked into the competition to build patent stockpiles and generate fees. Some have called licensing income an addiction, a mythological siren song that seduces otherwise intelligent CEOs."

As I note in Chapter 3, companies need to liberate IP value creation from the tyranny of balance sheet accounting, and look beyond the first-line dictionary definition of profit as "the gain in excess of expenditures." Instead, they should seek a broader definition of the profit to be gained from IP that includes the additional concepts of "useful consequences" and "valuable results." This would, of course, force CEOs into a more qualitative as opposed to quantitative decision-making arena, where (quite frankly) many fear to tread.

As Berman writes in *IAM:* "What is the value of a patent or family of patents that permit freedom to sell a product unencumbered? To slow a competitor? To facilitate a supply chain or a customer relationship?" The truth is, says Berman, "It is difficult [even] to pinpoint the role IP rights play in protecting products' market share or maintaining their profit margins. It is even more difficult to capture their impact on overall business performance."

Nevertheless, difficult is not impossible—and if nothing else, the 500-plus IP collaboration deals that Microsoft has signed with companies in the past six years demonstrates the sort of "valuable results" and "useful consequences" that can be gained when a company's senior leadership helps to guide IP value creation in a truly strategic manner. These collaborations—many forged by top Microsoft executives using IP as the glue cementing the deals together—have enabled Microsoft to pursue valuable joint product development opportunities with other firms, acquire needed outside technologies, disseminate more broadly and rapidly our own technologies and products into the market, bolster margins and market share, gain entry into new markets or broaden our freedom of action within a market, create joint sales and marketing opportunities with other companies for mutual benefit, and also generate some revenue directly through patent licensing.

In short, these IP-enabled collaborations have led to greater success for Microsoft in the marketplace, materially enhanced the company's bottom line, and advanced the interests of our shareholders. And that's in addition to IP's more traditional role in protecting Microsoft's most strategic technologies, helping us defend ourselves against the many patent hold-up suits filed against us every year, and ensuring that we generate as big a return as possible on the company's enormous investment in R&D.

Creating Real Business Value

In the words of Horacio Gutierrez (Microsoft's new chief intellectual property officer, or CIPO), "Our mission is to build, protect, and utilize the world's most valuable IP portfolio to create business value."

Which sounds simple enough. But as Gutierrez notes, "Creating business value is where the rub is. Because you can't really succeed at that if you treat IP as this sacred cow, as something you have to have because you've always had it, where it's just some budget line item with a few lawyers working on it to make sure that in case you're sued, you have something to fall back on."

He pauses a moment: "You know, when you realize that your IP is not a business objective of its own but a tool to advance the company's overall business objectives, that changes the kind of IP you get, what technologies you seek to protect, which countries you seek to protect it in, and how you use it. Do you keep it to yourself? Do you license it broadly? Do you give it away for free? Microsoft as well as every other company in the world has a number of choices about how to use its IP. But the overriding question is, Are you using it to advance the strategic objectives of the corporation?"

In the old days, when patents and other intellectual property served primarily as weapons of competitive warfare, that question was perhaps easier to answer. You focused mostly on leveraging IP's exclusivity value, using it either to block competitors in your market or at least "tax" them for the right to use your technology so that you could profit from their competition. But today's open innovation environment is incredibly more complicated to operate in. With breakthrough innovation now taking place across a broad array of companies, universities and even individuals—and with no one company able to accumulate by itself all the technologies and business competencies needed for success—companies now require mechanisms of collaboration so that they can combine their respective strengths to achieve that success. To be sure, you still need to differentiate your products and services from those offered by others, and that is still in most cases the primary function of your internal

R&D. But you can no longer be successful in today's world with a go-it-alone strategy.

As Gutierrez put it, "IP has a very important role in ensuring that companies have the ability to invest in developing differentiated products—features that my customers will want and that my competitors don't have. But that has to be balanced against the imperative to use IP as a vehicle for collaboration and greater interoperability in today's heterogeneous environment."

Which is why, he adds, "We have adopted a policy of licensing almost everything we invent to anyone on fair, reasonable, and reciprocal terms—with the exception of some intellectual property that has to do with the user interface, with the way our product looks and feels to the user, which is really our core brand and connection to the customer. We have one of the most open patent licensing policies of any company in the industry, and it has allowed us to innovate effectively while also giving us the ability to develop relationships and at times even tap into other people's innovations."

As an example, Gutierrez cites the technology of virtualization, which enables businesses to more seamlessly manage disparate computer hardware and software systems.

"A few years back," he explains, "it became clear that virtualization was going to become an important phenomenon in the industry—that it was going to catch on because of the value that it provides to customers in reducing the cost of their IT infrastructure and leveraging their existing hardware resources to run a variety of applications. So once we determined that this was going to be a trend in industry, we decided to invest more heavily in developing the technology and getting IP to protect our innovations in this space. This also required us to shift some resources away from other areas that weren't going to be as important going forward.

"So that was the first way that we tried to supply IP leadership on this front," he continues. "But then the other way we did it was in creating our patent and collaboration agreement with the Linux distributor Novell [see Chapter 4]. Virtualization is extremely important to major enterprises that use both Windows and Linux, and our cooperation together has led to some big advances in this area that have really benefited customers and both of our companies."

Gutierrez' remarks offer a portrait of the IP management function as an enabler of the business strategy and market objectives of the company—not a thing apart, although it does require a certain specific expertise to be effective in that role. The purpose of IP strategy, simply put, is to solve the technological and competitive problems of the business. It does this through a variety of complementary means—by anticipating the direction of technology and the market and making sure the company will have the freedom to innovate and compete in that future environment, by differentiating the company's products and services more effectively, and by facilitating partnerships and alliances that bring the company the outside technologies and market competencies it needs to succeed.

"The notion of an IP strategy that is divorced from the business strategy is just silly," insists Gutierrez. "To a large extent, the IP strategy *is* the business strategy."

At Microsoft, IP leadership is practical, not rhetorical. In every business unit, whenever there is a discussion of product or market strategy, there is a related IP discussion about what sort of IP is needed to enable that business to compete successfully, about how to allocate the resources to get the IP needed, and about what sort of IP landscape exists in which they will be competing—a map, essentially, of the IP challenges ahead. What patents are lurking out there among competitors that can cause problems? Does it make more sense to try to combine forces with a rival or to compete against it? What sort of licensing agreements, or patent cross-licensing agreements, or patent acquisitions, might be wise for the company to undertake?

These sorts of IP problem-solving discussions do not happen haphazardly, but are instead built into the organizational structure of the company. Very senior IP counsels are literally embedded within the business units and product teams. They are part of the extended leadership team of those business units, and their job is to figure out what sort of IP strategy will best support that group's business strategy. Every one of the company's business groups has the benefit of this sort of embedded IP expertise, and it is all managed and directed centrally through the IP&L team that Horacio Gutierrez has succeeded me in leading. IP counsel also work closely with Microsoft Research to ensure that the company is innovating for the future and not for only the next product cycle. And IP executives lead the IP Ventures group that "invests" some of the technology that doesn't get used in our products with startups and entrepreneurs so that we can be involved in new business opportunities created outside the company.

But as Gutierrez concedes, "There is only so much we would be able to do in the absence of senior executive endorsement and support for the IP function."

Leadership Must Start at the Top

Indeed, it would have been impossible for Microsoft to forge many of its most strategic IP collaboration deals without direct senior executive involvement. The negotiation of the breakthrough patent collaboration agreement with open source leader Novell—led personally by General Counsel Brad Smith with frequent input from CEO Steve Ballmer and Chairman Bill Gates—is an excellent case in point.

"The executive leadership of this company and the various business group leaders see IP as a powerful tool for achieving their objectives," says Gutierrez. "And we have been blessed here at Microsoft to have this kind of IP-savvy leadership, starting with Bill but extending really throughout the company."

Bill Gates himself is more modest about his role. "Yes, I think I've been more involved in patent stuff than most CEOs," he observes, "but that isn't the reason why this company is able to get up to 3,000 great patents a year and be an IP leader." Rather, he says, it's because the company is intensely innovative and spends the resources needed to support that effort—more than $7 billion a year, in fact, which is more than any other company on earth.

But Gates does agree, though, that "the CEO has got to set a tone and lead by example. You've got to encourage groups that are doing well. And you've got to give negative feedback to groups that aren't thinking about IP enough. The leadership has to do that, because otherwise the domain of being a researcher or an engineer or a lawyer or a business development executive is going to limit their vision only to the immediate tasks they face. So the leader has to bootstrap IP awareness throughout the company. And then it gets inculcated and becomes part of the culture."

If IP leadership doesn't start at the top, Gates believes, then a company may find itself making the same mistake that Xerox made with its Palo Alto Research Center. Founded in 1970, PARC was one of the two or three finest research laboratories in the world, and made a number of breakthrough inventions including laser printing, Ethernet networking technology, and the graphical user interface used in today's personal computers.

Unfortunately, Xerox's top executives failed to appreciate the value of the intellectual property being created at PARC, and as a result, allowed a host of other companies—including Apple and Microsoft—to reap the largest rewards from the commercialization of these inventions.

"They invested a lot in research," Bill explains, "but they didn't manage their IP well. So I think there's a lesson there for CEOs. At a lot of companies, it's only the legal department that gets involved in the IP issues. But not at Microsoft, because IP is central to who we are and what we do."

Yes, things really were a lot simpler in the old days, when intellectual property was seen merely as a "rights" issue rather than a business imperative. IP was left to the legal department to manage, and IP strategy was really just legal strategy—in short, the decision whether to litigate or license. Executive involvement was rare, and the IP organization, if indeed a formal one even existed, was composed solely of lawyers and perhaps a few licensing executives.

But today's open innovation environment, in which intellectual property is the company's single most valuable wealth-creating asset and its most effective tool for building collaborative relationships with other firms, complicates the task of IP leadership enormously.

For one thing, because intellectual property must now support the company's overall business strategy, its proper management must start at the senior-most levels of executive leadership and filter down into the activities of all the various business units and functional groups within the firm. In effect, the IP organization serves as a kind of "transmission belt" for strategic and tactical dialogue about IP between the executive suite and the business units dealing with their various R&D, marketing, business development, and communications challenges. And if the

IP group is to be effective in this role, it should be composed not only of attorneys but of business development, finance, M&A, marketing, licensing, and communications experts as well.

There's another reason to include people of diverse backgrounds in the IP team. As Frans Johannson points out in his 2006 book, *The Medici Effect*, many of the most crucial breakthrough insights in a field come from people with little or no related experience in it—from people who apply their past experience to a new and unfamiliar situation. Charles Darwin was a geologist when he proposed the theory of evolution. It was the astronomer Walter Alvarez who finally explained what happened to the dinosaurs. And in my own case, my background in international business, venture capital, and public policy helped me be open to new ideas in deploying IP for business success—whether that be IP acquisitions and investments, building relationships with venture capitalists and entrepreneurs through our IP Ventures program, or turning former enemies into friends through IP relationship-building, as we did with Novell.

Another example of how people of varied backgrounds can make breakthrough advances in the IP function involves George Zinn, originally a top guy in the finance department who I brought into IP&L. George was the person who first got us thinking about the company's IP assets from the perspective of a portfolio manager, helping to identify those that were underutilized and spurring us to devote greater efforts where greater gains could be made. After several years with us, he went on to become a corporate vice president and Microsoft's treasurer, bringing with him an awareness of IP as a wealth-creating asset that will benefit the company in all its operations.

Another challenge facing IP leaders is the question of *how* to lead. Precisely because IP managers need to develop close relations with the business leaders of the company and understand the day-to-day challenges they face, they need to become good advocates, educators, and especially listeners. Having a mandate from the CEO is all well and good, but what does a chief IP officer do in the not-uncommon case where the heads of the business units simply refuse to reply to his e-mails or phone calls? He can hardly go whine about it to the CEO, now can he?

Instead, he would do well to take another look at the classic 1938 treatise on leadership, "The Function of the Executive," by Chester L. Barnard. As Barnard points out, because many of the best ideas tend to flourish in the informal organization rather than in the hierarchy—and more to the point of our discussion, because IP managers today need to work with a wide range of people throughout the organization—the development and training of employees is of paramount importance, including around IP issues. Indeed, the IP manager's authority will rest upon his or her *ability to persuade* rather than to command.

Finally, because open (or collaborative) innovation involves the opportunistic leveraging of partnership prospects with other firms, IP leaders will have to embrace a degree of flexibility and an avoidance of rigid tactical roadmaps not experienced by previous generations of IP management.

"By definition, the use of IP to create strategic business value for a company requires a lot of nimbleness," Gutierrez believes, "if only because the market and the technology and the roster of who's a competitor and who's a partner is constantly changing. Companies that might be your competitors today could easily become your partners tomorrow. So as the whole company adapts to meet these changes, the IP strategy has to adapt as well."

Earlier, I quoted Nathan Myhrvold saying that the average grade for the executive management of patents and other intellectual property is a D-minus. Perhaps it would be more politic to say that throughout corporate America, the ability to create and leverage IP to advance a company's business interests is highly uneven, varying greatly from firm to firm. I cannot speak for the situation at every company. But what I can say is that when corporate IP professionals get together at meetings and conferences, the chief topics of discussion, while certainly pressing, are unfortunately often less than strategic: litigation exposure, cost management of the IP portfolio, benchmarking best practices in IP management, and other tactical and defensive issues, rather than strategic and proactive ones.

As IP managers, we really need to spend more time talking about the bigger picture. How do we use our IP team to help guide innovation strategy? How do we get in synch with and serve the business groups more effectively? Where's the industry going? What challenges are we going to face? How will we solve them?

Horacio Gutierrez offers an example: "How are we going to deal with mash-ups? How are we going to deal with 'cloud computing' and the emergence of a software-plus-services environment? How are we going to incentivize and protect the IP rights of content owners in a world of ubiquitous downloads that all get mixed and mashed together—not only from an enforcement perspective, but also from the perspective of creating a business model that makes sense both for consumers and for industry?"

Good question. We'll explore this and other issues in the next chapter.

Chapter 6

The Road Ahead
(with Apologies
to Bill Gates)

A merica and the world now face the worst economic
crisis in 80 years. Among the many other challenges
facing business leaders in the years ahead, one will be
the role that IP—and the innovation embodied in it—will play
in the revitalization of business and the economy.

To appreciate the possibilities, it's helpful to look back to
an earlier age—to the dawn of the industrial revolution and the
birth of the U.S. patent system itself—and examine the effects
America's unique IP regime had on what was then a backwater
agrarian economy.

Although most people don't realize it, America's Founding
Fathers did not simply create the world's first modern democratic republic. They also gave our young and fragile democracy,

through the creation of the world's first and only democratized patent system, the means by which it could succeed and prosper in a world dominated by much more powerful armies and economies.

The Founders very consciously set out to do this by constructing a patent system that would do what no other patent system had ever done before—namely, stimulate the inventive genius of the common man.

They did this first of all by enshrining for the first time anywhere in a nation's fundamental law—Article One of the U.S. Constitution—the obligation of government to "promote the progress of science and useful arts, by securing for limited times to authors and inventors the exclusive right to their respective writings and discoveries."

As nineteenth-century statesman Daniel Webster would later note, "The American Constitution does not attempt to give an inventor a right to his invention, or an author a right to his composition; it recognizes an original, pre-existing, inherent right of property in such invention or composition." This right, he added, "is, as a natural right, more than that which a man can assert in almost any other kind of property."

No other nation on earth before this had recognized what we now call intellectual property in this way; patents had heretofore always been a "favor" granted by the monarch or state.

But the real genius of the Founders in creating the conditions for future American greatness lay in the way they enabled this right to manifest itself in the everyday life of ordinary citizens. Their deeply-felt democratic ideals—hard to imagine today in our cynical age—led them to specifically reject the elitism of the British patent system, which charged exorbitant patent fees equal to 10 times the annual per capita income of its citizens. Instead, they reduced U.S. patent fees to a level that even ordinary workers and farmers could afford. They also greatly simplified administrative procedures for applying for a patent. And through other means as well—including allowing anyone applying for a patent by mail to do so postage-free—they created a patent system that encouraged innovation on a truly mass scale.

The results were dramatic—as Thomas Jefferson put it, the new American patent system has "given a spring to invention beyond my conception." Only 13 years after the first patent law was enacted by Congress in 1790, the United States had already surpassed Britain—until then the undisputed leader of the industrial revolution—in the number of new inventions patented. By 1860, the number of new inventions patented in the United States was an astonishing seven times the number in Britain.

The principal reason for this dramatic surge in American innovation, of course, was that by design the American patent system enabled and encouraged a much broader array of creative individuals to take part in inventive activity than was the case in Britain or other Old World countries. Whereas most of Britain's handful of inventors came from privileged backgrounds—who else, after all, could afford to dabble in inventive activity?—the vast majority of America's many thousands of inventors came from humble beginnings. They were farmers, factory workers, carpenters, and other artisans for the most part.

Indeed, of the 160 so-called "great inventors" of the nineteenth century, over 70 percent had only a primary or secondary school education. Half had little or no formal schooling at all. And many of the most famous names in American invention—men such as Matthias Baldwin (the locomotive), George Eastman (roll film), Elias Howe (the sewing machine), and

Thomas Edison (the electric light and the phonograph)—had left school at an early age to support their families.

What's interesting here is that the American patent system did not simply encourage the masses to participate in inventive activity. It made it *economically feasible* for them to do so. By granting large numbers of inventors secure property rights to their discoveries for a limited time, the patent system enabled the formation of the world's first-ever national marketplace for technology, in which inventors could license their patents, generate income, and in unprecedented numbers make a full-time career for themselves in innovation. This, of course, generated more invention.

Or, as Abraham Lincoln (himself a patentee) noted, the brilliance of the U.S. patent system was that it "added the fuel of interest to the fire of genius" latent among the masses of people.

In this first-ever national technology market, independent inventors "posted" announcements of their patented discoveries in publications such as *Scientific American* that were expressly founded for the purpose of disseminating information about new inventions. Commercial enterprises would then license or purchase patented inventions through this inventors' market and use them in their own internal product development.

Indeed, in those days the R&D departments of even the largest corporations bought the vast majority of their product technologies from this independent inventors' market. In 1894, for example, American Bell Telephone Company's R&D department licensed 73 patents from outside inventors, as compared to developing only 12 inventions from its own employees.

This corporate focus on externally sourced innovation was official policy at the time. As T. D. Lockwood, the head of American Bell Telephone's patent department, wrote to his board of directors in 1885, "I am convinced that it has never, is not now, and never will pay commercially to keep an establishment of professional inventors in our employ."

Indeed, it wasn't until the 1930s that the growing cost and complexity of technology—along with court rulings that finally allowed companies to enforce employment agreements that required employees to assign their inventions to the firm—drove companies to begin hiring staffs of in-house inventors. As a result, although independent inventors remained much-loved iconic figures symbolizing the best of Yankee ingenuity and our frontier, problem-solving spirit, the last 75 years has witnessed their marginalization as a force in corporate and national innovation efforts.

A Rebirth for Independent Inventors?

This is not to say that independent inventors haven't still been making notable contributions to industry and the consumer. The first patent for an implantable pacemaker was issued in 1962 to independent inventor Wilson Greatbatch. Frampton Ellis's athletic shoe, first patented in 1981, was eventually sold to Adidas. Shumpei Yamazaki's semiconductor innovations have been widely deployed by manufacturers. And of course Bill Gates of Microsoft, Steve Jobs and Steve Wozniak of Apple, and Linux originator Linus Torvalds also all began as independent inventor hobbyists, their discoveries leading to the creation of the personal computer and software industries.

But forces are now at work that appear to be reversing this "Schumpeterian decline" of independent inventors and leading to their rebirth as a newly potent force in global innovation. Indeed, the growing cost, complexity, and fragmentation of technology development that in the 1930s propelled the rise of in-house corporate R&D is now, ironically, having the opposite effect. And as knowledge becomes ever more widely distributed and technology innovation becomes increasingly dispersed and heterogeneous, a growing share of national innovation is once again taking place outside the centralized R&D labs of large firms among networks of innovators, including small companies and independent inventors.

Could today's irreversible trend of open innovation, combined with the emergence of the Internet as a global platform for knowledge exchange, open a very large door once again to independent inventors? Will companies follow the example of Microsoft's IP Ventures program (see Chapter 3) and go even further in collaborating with small firms and individual inventors? Will the iconic American independent inventor earn for himself a prominent place once again as an important figure in corporate innovation and product development?

There is evidence—some of it empirical, much of it anecdotal—to suggest that this may, in fact, be happening. The number of patents awarded to independent inventors, for example, increased by an estimated 30 percent between 1990 and 2000. Independent inventors were granted nearly 30,000 utility patents in 2001, or 18 percent of all U.S. utility patents. And as for whether or not they are actually commercializing their patented inventions, one study reported that nearly 40 percent of respondents to a survey of independent inventors had reported generating sales from their inventions, with about 20 percent of all respondents saying they had generated actual profits.

According to UCLA Professor Naomi Lamoreaux, America's foremost authority on the history and role of independent inventors in America, "The decline of independent inventors is reversing. And there is lots of research on this. Look at the studies of Silicon Valley by Anna Saxenian, studies of recent patenting behavior by Ashish Arora, studies of venture capital by Josh Lerner, and studies of large firms relying less on internal R&D by Richard Rosenbloom."

There is also plenty of anecdotal evidence to suggest that independent inventors are beginning to play a more prominent role in corporate innovation than they have in the past three-quarters of a century. The most obvious example, perhaps, is the success of the open source software produced by hundreds, if not thousands, of hobbyist developers. But the rising influence of independent inventors is visible in a variety of fields.

In a January 9, 2006 article in *BusinessWeek* on "collaborative innovation," for example, IBM executive Linda Sanford wrote: "No company today can corner the market on innovation. For the first time ever, we have the luxury of a global market for brainpower—largely because of the Internet—and this talent does not have to be on the payroll for a company to leverage it."

She cites as an example the drug giant Eli Lilly's Web-based InnoCentive program, which created a virtual talent pool of more than 50,000 scientists in 150 countries. "Lilly posts R&D problems any scientist can tackle if he or she has the right expertise," Sanford explains. "The success rate has been far higher than in-house performance, at around one-sixth of the cost of doing it all in-house."

The bottom line, writes Sanford, is that the open innovation forces at work that are dispersing and fragmenting technology development "have leveled the playing field, giving companies *and individuals* [emphasis added] new power to compete globally."

But whatever the future of independent inventors—and I personally think it is bright—what is indisputable is that the world's first democratized patent system bequeathed to us by our Founders was the crucial engine that powered our industrial growth in the nineteenth century and made us the preeminent economic superpower that we are today. So effective was the U.S. patent system in spurring economic growth, in fact, that Europe and Japan reformed their own IP regimes along similar lines. The result is that today, the global intellectual property system has become the most effective spur to innovation and economic growth ever designed by man.

Don't Eat Your Seed Corn

Nations, companies, and citizens everywhere would be wise to bear this history in mind as they consider the economic, regulatory, and other reforms required to survive the current downturn and emerge with our core engines of future growth and prosperity not only intact but reinvigorated.

Regulate business and the financial markets more stringently? Who can possibly argue with that anymore? Spend what it takes to get people back to work and keep them in their homes, while laying the groundwork now for some serious deficit reduction a few years down the road? Absolutely! Tighten our corporate and governmental belts wherever we can? That's just common sense.

But let's make sure we don't eat our own seed corn in the process. Don't cut back on innovation spending—the lifeblood of business growth and future national prosperity—and don't take a hatchet to the intellectual property system when more modest surgical corrections would produce a far better result.

I mention this because, as everyone knows, there are many justified complaints of the patent system today, especially in the United States. Perhaps they can best be summarized in the following quote:

The Road Ahead (with Apologies to Bill Gates)

The quality of patents has suffered, many are neither novel nor useful. And the courts are overwhelmed by patent infringement and validity suits.

Now, what's really fascinating about that statement is that it was actually uttered in 1836 by a U.S. senator named John Ruggles, who authored the Patent Act of that year, which was the first of several major reforms of the patent system.

And therein lies an important point: whenever the United States has undergone a major industrial renaissance—such as occurred during the nineteenth century when first steam and then later the telegraph, telephone, and electric power industries emerged—the number of new patents have skyrocketed, as have concerns about a resulting decline in patent quality and an increase in patent litigation. So in 1836, and again in 1870, Congress reformed the patent system to better enable it to meet the demands of new technologies and new industries.

Today's renaissance boom in information age technology has once again strained our patent system. The PTO simply hasn't had the resources to respond to the three-fold increase in patent applications over the past 20 years. And as a result, patent quality has suffered in some areas and litigation rates have risen. Hence the need once again for reforms to help the patent system meet the challenges of today's new technologies and new industries.

Patent quality must be improved. We must make it easier for small businesses and independent inventors to obtain patents for their discoveries. We must take reasonable steps to reduce the flood of litigation. And we need to harmonize our patent system with those of other countries. This last item is perhaps the most important measure we could take in the short term, for it is incredibly inefficient and expensive for applicants to conduct prior art searches and obtain patents in each and every country separately.

But there are voices today—in some cases, very loud voices—for whom reform is not enough. They argue that intellectual property is outmoded, a tool used by monopolists to crush innovative young firms, and a barrier to open innovation, knowledge sharing, and economic growth. They cloak their arguments in the rhetoric of "the common good." But some of their misguided proposals—such as their call to eliminate patent rights for software or to abrogate IP rights in order to achieve greater interoperability—would, if adopted, cut the heart out of the knowledge economy and lead to devastating losses in jobs and living standards for millions worldwide.

To be sure, their critique of the intellectual property system is often framed as a battle between rich and poor, between the developed world and the developing world. But nothing could be further from the truth. In fact, more than 100 years of economic research around the world has proved beyond any doubt that the intellectual property system remains a breathtakingly effective spur to innovation and economic growth in all nations, rich and poor.

We know, for example, that patented technology innovation accounts for up to half the growth of the entire U.S. economy. And looking at my own industry—software—in particular, we can see that since patenting began in this sector 15 years ago, the software industry has exploded from only 1 percent to over 10 percent of total U.S. R&D. Yet, interestingly, studies also show that the software industry is still far less monopolized—and far more open to entrepreneurial innovation—than the average U.S. industry. In fact, there are many more new startups entering the software industry today than there were before patenting began. IP rights, clearly, have spurred innovation.

And IP's role in promoting innovation and growth is hardly limited to the United States. Intellectual property rights in software are now essential to the jobs and living standards of tens of millions of people the world over. Of the 1.2 trillion dollars spent worldwide on information technology this year, 21 percent of that will go towards software. Yet that 21 percent produces more than half of the 35 million jobs worldwide in the information technology sector.

Overall throughout the world, patenting produces an average increase in R&D investment of around 6 percent. And the trade in ideas made possible through international patent licensing is now growing at twice the rate of the trade in goods.

Indeed, in every country studied—whether rich or poor— economists have found that it is not capital resources or infrastructure or education, but rather the strength of a country's intellectual property system, that is the primary spur to technology development and economic growth. As one European study noted, in the absence of strong intellectual property rights, "The leading countries have insufficient incentive to invent and the follower countries have excessive incentive to copy," rather than invent for themselves.

In past decades, for example, the intellectual property system was a major catalyst for the development of indigenous technology by Korean companies, several of which have become global market leaders. Korea's amazing transformation from a poor farming economy in the 1960s with a per capita income of less than $100 to a highly industrialized country with a per capita income of more than $12,000 today resulted from a systematic economic and trade development policy that included intellectual property incentives at its core.

Today, IP's ability to spark innovation and growth in developing nations is perhaps most dramatically evident in China.

There, the number of new patented inventions is growing by an astonishing 30 percent or more each year. In the last five years, in fact, the number of active patents has doubled to more than 850,000. Indeed, China now has even more patent applications than the United States. And their international patent applications are growing by a staggering 500 percent per year.

It is no accident, of course, that as a result of this surge in IP activity, China's total R&D spending is now growing at a phenomenal 25 percent per year—the highest rate of growth in R&D investment of any nation on earth.

One result of this development is that piracy and counterfeiting in China is no longer just an enforcement issue to be addressed by external pressure from outside governments and multinational firms. For the first time, there are now strong *internal forces* encouraging the protection and strengthening of intellectual property rights, including a nationwide government education campaign on the benefits of IP.

As one recent European study noted, "There is intensified demand by Chinese companies for stronger IP rights domestically and for [building] collaborative IP [relationships] abroad."

Ten years from now, the biggest IP nations in the world (in terms of the number of patent applications) will in all likelihood no longer be the United States or Japan or the European nations, but rather China and other developing countries. That's because they are seeing with their own eyes the growth in their local economies that comes from encouraging innovation through the establishment of strong and fair intellectual property systems.

That said, I still believe that the United States—if it plays its cards right—will continue to maintain its science and technology leadership in the years ahead. A recent report by the U.S. National Intelligence Council highlighted a whole range of factors that shape a country's innovation and economic growth potential—these range from the nation's fluidity of capital and the flexibility of the labor pool to education, cultural propensity to encourage creativity and the strength of its intellectual property system. The report concluded that while China and other developing nations were indeed making great strides in all areas of innovation and growth, "the United States is expected to remain dominant in three areas: protection for intellectual property rights, business sophistication to mature innovation, and encouragement of creativity."

In the words of Joff Wild, the respected editor of *Intellectual Asset Management* magazine, "I do not see how China and India can fulfill their potential until they are able to match the U.S. on IP. And not just in the narrow legal sense, but in the whole process of turning innovation into something quantifiable and exploitable. In other words, developing the means to spot IP creation opportunities so as to create portfolios that add significant value to [a company's] bottom line and to the national economy."

What's really remarkable about the current debate over IP's role in economic development is that it's almost exactly the same debate that took place 50, and then again 150 years ago. In each of those periods, just as now, dramatic upsurges in innovation led to problems with patent quality and increasing litigation as patent offices worldwide struggled to adapt to a huge increase in patent applications. And in each period, as well, a few of those calling for reform wanted to throw out the baby with the bathwater, arguing that the intellectual property system itself hindered progress and amounted to the legalized granting of "monopolies" that were injurious to the public interest.

In his *Principles of Political Economy*, published in 1848, the liberal British philosopher and parliamentarian John Stuart Mill argued strongly against this view: "The condemnation of monopolies ought not to extend to patents, by which the originator of a new process is permitted to enjoy, for a limited period, the exclusive privilege of using his own improvement," wrote Mill. "This is not making the commodity dearer for his benefit, but merely postponing a part of the increased cheapness (or excellence) which the public owe to the inventor, in order to compensate and reward him for his service."

Or, as the American historian of the patent office, George H. Knight, asked around the same time: "How can the exclusive right of an invention be compared with a monopoly in trade? How can the exclusive privilege to sell salt in Elizabeth's time—which added not one bushel to the production, but which enriched the monopolist and robbed the community—and the exclusive right of Whitney to his cotton gin, which has added hundreds of millions to the products and exports of the country, be both branded, with equal justice, with the odious name of monopoly?"

And in 1864, the famed French jurist and economist Louis Wolowski, chair of industrial economics at the Conservatoire des Arts et Métiers, also replied to the charge of monopoly: "The dawn of the right of inventors has actually been contemporaneous with the destruction of monopolies odious to the common justice of men," he wrote. "Their rights, under patents, are called 'monopolies' only from the poverty of language, which has failed to express in words a distinction which no less clearly exists."

Beyond the (mostly) false charges of "monopoly," what critics of the IP system fail to recognize is its incredible resilience and adaptability in continuing to spur innovation and economic growth through changing economic conditions. Like the American democratic system itself, which has adapted over more than 200 years to meet each new challenge, the intellectual property system created by our Founders—a system now embraced in large degree by the majority of countries in the world—has also stood the test of time and proven its worth to mankind.

Of Transparency, Clouds, and Other Visions

Today, new and complex challenges confront the world's intellectual property regimes.

Will the current economic crisis and the plummeting value of tangible assets, for example, finally compel hard-pressed businesses to more effectively liberate their intangible IP assets and disclose with greater transparency their impact on corporate performance to investors, thus restoring some measure of confidence?

With the emergence of "cloud" computing and mash-up innovation, how can patent licensing encourage rather than stifle the development of new products and services?

In a world where distinctions between open source and proprietary software are becoming increasingly irrelevant, what role can IP play in facilitating greater collaboration within the industry for the benefit of businesses and customers alike?

And finally, in a world of ubiquitous Internet downloads and user-generated content, how can copyright continue to encourage the creation of quality media of all types without restricting user access to the news and information they want?

Regarding the first issue—the challenges facing IP managers posed by the current economic crisis—there is a great deal of talk nowadays about the need to finally get the huge percentage of all corporate value represented by IP assets on the balance sheet so that the executive suite can better manage it and investors can better understand this hitherto hidden factor in corporate performance. But although greater transparency in corporate affairs and in the financial markets is certainly needed—and despite the fact that the Securities and Exchange Commission (SEC), the Financial Accounting Standards Board (FASB), and virtually every other responsible regulatory and intellectual property authority has advocated it—no one seems to truly know how to make this happen. So little if any progress has been made.

The reasons why greater transparency in reporting IP's enormous impact on corporate performance remains so elusive—and why it remains so difficult to create more effective markets for IP, the most valuable asset class of our era—are mind-numbingly complex and, in any event, beyond the scope of this book. But perhaps one small indicator of the challenges that the business, financial, and regulatory community face here is to simply consider the differing valuation paradigms for a tangible asset like a house as compared to an intangible asset like a patent.

A house, after all, is worth what it's worth no matter who lives in it—and its worth can be more or less determined through comparables. The worth of a patent, on the other hand, depends upon who wants to use it, for what commercial or other purpose, in what market (or litigation setting), and under what set of economic and legal constraints.

That said, I do believe that as investors increasingly realize the centrality of intellectual property to corporate performance, companies will inevitably begin to develop some form of IP reporting to accompany their traditional financial disclosures. This can include, among other things, a narrative summary that describes the company's basic business model, plan and strategy, and then shows how IP contributes to the bottom line of the enterprise. What were the returns from IP-protected business segments? Does your IP portfolio help you secure or bolster your market share and profits, and if so by how much? Does the company have in place a systematic process for managing and exploiting its IP assets? Is it leveraging its IP portfolio to develop partnerships and product- or market-development collaborations with other firms, and how are those contributing to overall company performance? Does the IP of competitors pose a threat to any of the firm's lines of business?

These are just some of the questions that future investors will want answered about an asset class that materially affects the performance and future prospects of firms in which they are considering investing. And if corporate executives and boards finally decide to more effectively manage this critical asset class so as to maximize returns to shareholders, I do believe that, in time, we will see much more useful reporting and more effective disclosure of IP's role in business. This will, just as the development by Paconi in 1494 of double-entry bookkeeping did, inevitably reduce the cost of capital, bolster investor confidence, and spur greater innovation and economic growth.

Another challenge facing business and IP leaders is the emergence of "cloud" computing, in which software and services reside in the Internet and then are served to a multiplicity and diversity of client devices. What questions does that raise?

For one thing, it generates questions regarding interoperability—how do we ensure that all those various devices work well with each other? The promise of new technology, after all, is to provide the user with a seamless experience using whatever device he or she wants.

And to be sure, interoperability is a technical challenge. But it's not only a technical challenge. It's also an intellectual property challenge.

How, for example, do companies maintain the incentive to keep innovating in a world in which their products and services will be mixed and matched by consumers with all kinds of other companies' products and services—sometimes resulting in still new products and services built atop the mash-up of everyone else's products and services? The challenge will be to facilitate this creative patchwork of existing innovations without killing the incentive for further innovation—meaning, without destroying your ability to profit from that portion of the consumer mash-up that represents your own products and services. One thing that's going to require is some creativity in developing new kinds of IP licenses.

Microsoft's VP of IP and Licensing Horacio Gutierrez explains: "A lot of what we're asking ourselves today is, What role can we play in being creative around IP issues that can help enable that new world to come into being in the best way for everyone? How do we do this in a way that respects other people's IP, that reduces everyone's exposure to infringement claims, but that ultimately gives the consumer all the content and software and services in a way that is seamless and painless, so that it doesn't matter what device or content provider they're using?"

Gutierrez shrugs: "Now some people might say, 'Just give up the IP. Let's agree to create a no-IP zone in the mash-up cloud.' Well, that would certainly solve a lot of the problems, just like making food free would also solve a lot of problems—but only in the short run. Who is going to produce more food tomorrow if they can't make a living from it?"

Gutierrez believes that while there are obviously no easy answers to this question, there are some historical examples that should at least inspire hope that IP solutions will be developed. He cites, for example, the challenge faced by music copyright owners with the advent of mass-market radio, when it suddenly became impossible to know how many times, and in what markets, a particular song had been played. So collecting societies emerged such as ASCAP, the American Society of Composers, Authors, and Publishers, that organized scientific surveys and built statistical models that enabled them to approximate the number of times a song had been played and collect royalties for the copyright holders. It may not have been a perfect solution, but it was a workable one in the sense that the American public got to hear the music it wanted to hear and the creators of that music were able to earn a living that enabled them to keep creating music.

"I'm not saying that collecting societies are the answer to the mash-up problem," Gutierrez insists. "But I am saying that we have in the past been faced with similar problems of new technology and increased scale concerning IP issues. And so far, at least, we've always been able to develop workable IP solutions to those problems. So the role of IP leaders in companies is not to keep looking at the way the world was or the way the world is, but to be creative in thinking about problems that we're going to face in the world of tomorrow."

A third challenge confronting IP leaders involves the future of open source software development and its impact on the intellectual property strategies of businesses. On this issue, one thing is indisputably clear: the old ideological divide between open source and proprietary software has blurred to the point of near-invisibility as businesses of all types increasingly ship "mixed source" products containing both kinds of software.

Hard-core free software ideologues may rail against this fact—and boy, do they ever!—but their complaints are now beginning to take on the futile air of old-time utopian socialist entreaties about them.

"The new application [in data centers] is a mixture of [proprietary] and open source applications and it's going to stay that

way in the future," argues Russell Pavlicek, a senior Linux architect with Cassatt Corp. in San Jose, California. "That's resulted
in fewer licensing costs and issues, and given IT managers greater
control over software development. This is the reality of history;
the trend is established."

The trend toward mixed source software is irreversible
precisely because it is being propelled by economic reality. In
recent years, not only has the development of new software applications exploded, but the amount of software in hardware
products has also risen dramatically as devices gained more func-
tionality through software. All this has driven up the cost of
software development, and in response, software vendors have
outsourced part of their development efforts, mixing and match-
ing open source and proprietary code from a variety of sub-
contractors to reduce costs and speed time to market for their
products.

But another factor that is erasing the old open source versus proprietary software divide is the continuing evolution of
open source businesses themselves. As Chapter 4 discusses, at
least 67 percent of new additions to the Linux kernel are
contributed by corporate employees rather than pure hobbyist developers—some sources now say that figure has risen to
85 percent—and open source companies are increasingly adding
proprietary features of their own to increase the value-add of
their products. In fact, according to Matt Aslett, the open source
business analyst for the 451 Group and someone who has done
some really smart thinking on this issue, 50 percent of open
source vendors are employing a hybrid mixed-source development model today—and 60 percent are using traditional commercial licensing models to generate their revenue.

In other words, the distance between the "Cathedral and
the Bazaar" has narrowed to the point where, just as with the

distance between cities and suburbs, meaningful distinctions have become increasingly difficult to discern.

Not that software holy warriors like Richard Stallman and Eben Moglen don't keep trying. Following Microsoft's historic agreement with open source leader Novell, they and their cohorts revised the open source general public license (GPL)—the first such revision in over 15 years—to specifically forbid the kind of patent covenant-not-to-sue agreed to by Microsoft and Novell. Indeed, if you read their documents and presentations, you can see that they specifically designed the update from GPLv2 to GPLv3 with "get Microsoft" and "get Novell" provisions in mind.

The problem for these free software die-hards is that, because the new GPLv3 is entirely voluntary, most open source companies have refused to adopt it and continue to use the older GPLv2. Even Linux creator Linus Torvalds—the "father" of the modern open source movement—has publicly opposed GPLv3's effort to block collaboration between the two software models.

Indeed, says Torvalds, this new license makes the split clear between what he calls the "religious beliefs" of Stallman and Moglen's Free Software Foundation and the goal of the majority of open source developers to create great software for customers.

In any event, mixed source software has become such a fact of life in the industry that whole new businesses have arisen, including Black Duck Software, to help companies developing such software manage the complex intellectual property clearances they need.

What's next on the horizon? We should probably not expect another historic agreement of the kind that Microsoft and Novell worked out—although another attempt by Microsoft and Red Hat to collaborate on patent and interoperability matters would certainly attract a lot of attention within the industry and be warmly welcomed by both companies' customers. Rather, the next few years are likely to witness the development of improved licensing models that free developers and customers from IP concerns and reduce the cost of development for all software companies—mixed source, proprietary, and open source alike.

Just Say No to the "Free Content" Farce

Moving finally to the challenge posed by online media and user-generated content, the good news may be that here, at least, the problem that needs to be surmounted is absolutely clear—the "free content" model of publishing on the Internet simply doesn't work, at least for publishers. It's a dead-end.

This was the rather bold argument advanced by Microsoft's Chief Counsel for Intellectual Property Strategy, Tom Rubin, in his address to the Association of Online Publishers in the United Kingdom on November 20, 2008. So far as I know, Rubin is one of only two individuals—the other I'll quote shortly—to have the guts to finally call out the "elephant in the room" regarding the free-content model of publishing pushed by Google and others.

In his remarks, Rubin said it was high time for the media to end this self-defeating charade that "information wants to be free" and instead demand their fair share of the billions in profit that search engines and news aggregators are earning from their content. Unless they do, Rubin argued, the high-quality journalism and the independent media that the citizens of a free society require may not survive much longer.

And there is no doubt that journalism and publishing are facing a life-threatening crisis. As Rubin and a host of analysts have noted, revenues and profits are down across the industry, and as Rubin puts it, "staff and resource cutbacks are cutting the very heart out of investigative reporting and other quality journalism operations."

So what can be done to save publishing? The first step, Rubin insists, is to reject the myth that we are simply passive spectators to the process of technological change. While we can't stop new technology, he says—nor, given its obvious benefits, should we even want to—history proves, as he puts it, that "we most certainly *can* shape the way it is deployed. Our own recent history proves that the free-content, copyright-be-damned approach is not inevitable at all."

"Remember Napster?" he asks. "When this music downloading service was launched back in 1999,the pundits insisted that the music industry must inevitably bow before this technological advance. But that didn't happen. Instead, Napster was found liable for massive copyright infringement, and had to shut down. In its place, music industry and technology executives collaborated on a new and better model—represented by Apple's iTunes music store—that sells digital music files to eager customers with the permission of their copyright owners. It turned out that most people do not want to steal music—they just want affordable and convenient online access to it."

Rubin also cites the example of Google's Book Search service, which started scanning books into its digital database a few years ago without first getting permission from the copyright owners. Authors and book publishers eventually sued Google for copyright infringement, and in October of 2008, they won a $125 million settlement from Google.

Writing about this settlement, the editor and media critic Peter Osnos had this to say: "Google has now conceded, with a very large payment, that information is *not* free."

Osnos then went on to ask the questions that, apparently, no one else in media circles had had the courage to ask before. "Why aren't newspapers and news magazines demanding payment for use of their stories on Google and other search engines? Why are they not getting a significant slice of the advertising revenues generated by use of their stories via Google?" And why, Osnos asked, are news proprietors "unable to do what book publishers and authors did and take on Google for what is an absolutely core issue of fairness—and increasingly, of survival?"

Good questions all. And as Tom Rubin argued in his speech, the core solution to today's crisis in publishing lies in developing a more sustainable media ecosystem for the Internet age that is built upon the three bedrock principles—he calls them the "Three Cs"—of *copyright, competition,* and *collaboration.*

"First," Rubin insisted, "journalists, authors, and publishers must reclaim from search engines the control of their own branded, copyrighted content. Second, the online publishing business must remain free and competitive, with plenty of room for new creators to emerge, and with no single entity—be it a publisher or a technology company—able to gain a chokehold over revenue streams or reader experiences. And third, publishers and technology companies must collaborate to ensure that the great promise of our digital age is realized in ways that preserve and enhance the quality journalism that any free society depends upon."

Clearly, Rubin has done a lot of good thinking on this subject, and I couldn't agree with him more when he says, "Don't let anyone tell you that the choice is between Luddite resistance to new technology and passive acquiescence to the destruction of the media industry." There is, indeed, a better way to serve the needs of users for convenient online access to quality content and at the same time nurture the continued creation of that content.

What is hopefully clear in this discussion is that as technology evolves, intellectual property strategies must evolve with it. We have already seen a huge evolution in IP strategy just in the last decade, as the emergence of the open innovation era transformed IP from primarily a weapon of competitive warfare into a bridge to collaboration between firms.

IP's role will continue to evolve—indeed, must evolve—to meet the demands of new technologies and changing economic realities, continually recalibrating IP's careful balance between private incentive and public interest. That is the only way intellectual property can continue, as it has for the past 200-plus years, to serve as a spur to innovation and economic progress that benefits the whole of society.

Index

179

Index

Index

Index